New

W9-BVC-265

REBIRTH

of a

DREAM

A Young Black
Man's Fearless
Mission to Resurrect
His Father's Vision

REBIRTH
of a
DREAM

A Young Black
Man's Fearless
Mission to Resurrect
His Father's Vision

m&p | MCKENZIE & PORTER
PUBLISHING

Omaha, Nebraska

EAN GARRETT

© 2012 Ean Garrett

All rights reserved. No part of this book may be used or reproduced in any manner whatsoever without written permission except in the case of brief quotations embodied in critical articles or reviews. For publishing inquiries, address McKenzie & Porter Publishing, McKenzie and Porter Publishing PO Box 183, Omaha, NE 68101, 402-884-5995.

This book is a personal story and is not intended to be a source for any type of medical advice, legal counsel, or other professional guidance. If you need help, it is your responsibility to seek advice from the appropriate professional. Author has obtained permission from persons mentioned (or their families) to share their stories, or has used pseudonyms and changed other identifying information for the protection of certain individuals. Products or services mentioned herein are the property of their respective trademark, service mark, or copyright owners and are designated so by this statement. The author holds no responsibility or liability for the performance or non-performance of any product, service, or organization mentioned herein.

ISBN13: 978-1-936840-11-3

Library of Congress Control Number: 2012936335

Author's Note: The people and incidents described in this book are real. In a few cases names have not been used to preserve anonymity. The original poetry was written for this book.

Printed in the USA.

10   9   8   7   6   5   4   3   2   1

CONTENTS

How did I meet Ean Garrett? At the time, I was the CEO of MENTOR: The National Mentoring Partnership, and we were deep in the process of planning for an upcoming series of events. We had reached the point in the event planning cycle that produces either panic or euphoria: we were exploring the list of available speakers. One slot left unfilled called for a young person who was involved in a mentoring relationship and who had both the willingness and ability to talk to a very large audience.

At that moment in the discussion, colleague James Waller walked into the room, interrupted our work session and said, "You've got to meet this kid from Nebraska."

That kid was fifteen-year-old Ean Garrett, who went on to speak to the audience assembled in New York for MENTOR's 2002 National Recognition Event. Here's how Ean concluded his remarks:

From the start I was expected to lose. Everything I have right now is mostly because I defied what the world concluded about me before I could even speak a word in my defense. And my defense is that I am just as capable as any person to do great things. Like you, I think about all the things this world could achieve if every child were given the right tools. Mentoring is the right tool and it is the way to their own "American Dream." I hope you will promise to do all everything you can to help make mentoring and the American Dream a reality for every child in this city and every other city in the country. It's their best defense, too.

While all in the audience were touched by Ean's poise, passion, and the particulars of his personal odyssey, I was impressed by something else as well. Ean's remarks focused on himself only insofar as needed to make an authentic, unapologetic plea for all the young people who found themselves in the same hard place as he. From that moment on, I've never failed to be impressed by the young boy Ean was and the young man he has become.

As you read this book, my bet is that you will not only be equally impressed, you will be moved by the story of a boy whose early years were marked by a series of devastating blows. Odds makers will tell you that any one of them—the murder of his father; the drug dependency and subsequent rehabilitation of his mother; the inability of a foster-care system to help rather than harm—was likely to have consigned Ean to a future few of us would regard as worth having. Instead, Ean found his way to sources of help, asked for help, and kept asking until he got what he needed to get to where he knew he could go.

Today, Ean Garrett is a new graduate of the University of Nebraska Law School just about to embark on a career that delivers on his dreams and honors the achievements of the father he never got the chance to know. Let him tell you how he managed to do this. You are sure to be struck by how very much it takes to beat the odds makers and appalled that this is so. You are sure, too, to appreciate the remarkable persistence and extraordinary kindness of heart that makes his hard-won insights worth serious attention. And, finally, you are certain to leave the experience as grateful as I was for an introduction to Mr. Ean Garrett, Esquire.

Gail Manza
CEO, MENTOR

INTRODUCTION

It was my father's dream to escape the strongholds of poverty and to defy the world's dismal expectations of him as a Black man in America. It was his dream that by pure circumstance I came to adopt as my own. I wasn't perfect and made multiple mistakes along the way. But through me the beauty of my father's dream has been reborn, and through these pages it is my hope that it lives forever.

The first pages of this book were written long before my existence. This book is a culmination of the trials and triumphs of myself and my father before me. I was inspired to write this book in order to reach out to anyone who has ever had a dream. It is also my purpose to give the reader a micro-view of the journey of a lower-class Black youth in America, from the perspective of a Black youth.

Born in the winter of 1952 on Abraham Lincoln's birthday, my father was raised in a small Iowa town called

Council Bluffs, demographically no different from any other quiet town in Middle America. Located directly across the Missouri River from Omaha, Nebraska, the small town had been a key stopping point for early migrants seeking a new life in the West.

Fairly short with a solid frame and a light complexion, my father was often described as extremely personable. He was the youngest of four children, with two of his siblings sharing a different father. He grew up in one of the only Black families in his small town during an era where the country was deeply divided over the issue of race. Yet, his infectious personality provided him with the ability to transcend racial divides while still maintaining strong cultural roots.

My grandmother possessed a deep brown skin tone with strong facial features and was loved dearly by most who were lucky enough to have known her. She worked as a maid for various white families throughout the community, which provided her with a meager income to help support her own family. My grandfather, on the other hand, was bi-racial—his mother Black and his father white. He was short with a light complexion and very distinct freckles that dotted his entire face.

No one had any idea who my grandfather's biological father was, and in our family the slightest mention of the subject was taboo. He was born in the early thirties, so the mystery and controversy surrounding my grandfather's lineage had underlying hints of a painful past. As a result there were few questions regarding how he came to be; rather it was simply accepted that he was. He took any odd jobs that he could find to make ends meet. My grandparents were hardworking people yet still remained poor, and neither had ever been formally educated beyond high school.

Usually a time filled with joyful smiles and gladness, holidays would prove to be some of the most trying of times for my father and his family. Christmas would be an especially difficult time. On more than one occasion, my father received nothing more than a belt and used socks that my grandmother had obtained from the white families she worked for. She would sew up any holes in the socks and give them to my father and his siblings. Like most hardworking families in their position, they tried to make the most of what they had. Such experiences were merely preliminary tests of faith, unknowingly preparing my father's inner strength for what obstacles lay ahead.

Due to ailing health that had finally defeated her, my grandmother passed away tucked in a hospital bed, while my father had barely begun high school. She had been the backbone of the family, a matriarch, and her death while still in her forties deeply affected my father who cherished her beyond description.

At this time my father was the only sibling who still had not yet left home. His older siblings had already embarked on their own optimistic journeys to discover their young adulthoods. Left alone with his father, who had been known for being an alcoholic and verbally abusive, my father endured.

After my grandmother's death, my grandfather allowed his drinking friends to move in. Soon my father became unimportant—like a list of things that can wait until one feels the inclination to get around to it. His father would often sit in the living room with his friends and eat a hearty meal, while my father was forced to watch as if invisible with nothing left to eat. Still, he continued to remain focused during his senior year of high school and would break ground as the first Black senior class president of his predominantly white high school.

During my father's freshman year of college, his father's lifeless remains had been discovered at home in his recliner long after rigor mortis had set in. Another unexpected death half caused by a broken heart at the death of my grandmother and partly by the liquor my grandfather would often use to fill the endless void. Having both parents pass away in such a short period of time naturally came to take its toll on my father and his siblings. After their passing my father would be taken in by close friends of the family.

When they took in my father, "Big Mama" and "Big Daddy" were already well known throughout the community for providing a home for wards of the state and children who were victims of unfortunate circumstances. Big Mama was slender with ivory skin. Her name was a perfect reflection of her commanding presence as she efficiently ran the family with a zero tolerance for nonsense. She had long silver hair and would sway back and forth on an old rocking chair, seemingly intent on times few still were alive to give a living account of. Big Daddy had a good job working on the railroads and was also a World War II veteran.

While living with Big Mama and Big Daddy, my father became extremely close to a girl they adopted, whom I would later come to know as Aunt Mary Ann. With a smooth brown skin tone and a sharp intellect, she had been one of five children who were all the product of an extramarital affair. After her mother had given all of her brothers and sisters up for adoption, she had found her way into the home of Big Mama and Big Daddy. She not only would come to play a significant role in the life of my father but she later would play an instrumental role in mine as well.

Living in a new and stable environment provided my father with a firm platform from which to excel. He would go on to attend Luther College in Decorah, Iowa, on a full academic scholarship. After graduating from Luther College in three years, he attended Creighton University Law School in Omaha, Nebraska, with hopes of helping those in the local community who were also from disadvantaged backgrounds.

It was his goal to use law school as a stepping stone not only to help the less fortunate, but also as a way to escape poverty himself. Eventually, after obtaining his law degree, he decided to start his own law practice at the age of twenty-seven. While constantly taking on numerous pro bono cases, he spent the rest of his life fighting for the downtrodden and systematically oppressed.

His upbringing was highly untraditional but still far from unique. Millions of Black youth in the United States continue to face poverty. According to figures released by the Urban Institute as recently as June 2010, 77 percent of Black children experience poverty at some point during their childhood, while a third will remain poor throughout their youth.

In hindsight, my father was faced with a choice whether to be overwhelmed by his situation or to escape it, and he chose emancipation. With his success he was able to help those around him, while serving as a model of upward mobility.

I think that it is important to acknowledge how people react differently to adversity. Adversity can either break you or empower you. Often the harsh realities that we face each day are too overwhelming for some to adjust, and life ends up getting the best of them. The easiest way to instantly escape any unfavorable reality is to dream. It is only through our dreams that we can alter reality and ultimately accomplish our ambitions.

On Christmas morning when all that was under my father's tree was a pair of used socks and a belt, I believe my father dreamed of more. I imagine that at night when he went to sleep hungry, he dreamed of being full. I'm sure that in his dreams he pictured his children never having to experience the hard times that he did. I can vividly envision him lying on his back in his bed staring past the ceiling, while being kept awake by a burning desire to taste the fruits of his own ambition.

Regardless of what your economic or ethnic background is, most individuals desire economic stability and the opportunities that only hard work can bring. With a fair shot at upward mobility, it is inconceivable what one can achieve. My father held on to a dream to surpass what little was expected of a demographic long neglected.

With an unpredictable twist of fate, my father's dream would be one that I too incidentally would come to share. It would become the resurrection of an obsessive determination to overcome, stemming from a child's desperate vision shrouded in optimism. I guess you could call it the rebirth of a dream. This is my story.

Infinite souls stand in a long line in the presence of the
divine, while waiting for one's ticket to be torn; such is the
genesis of the unborn.

Fearing most abortion, hoping to be fathered by fame and
fortune, many will be newborn victims of chance nursed by
unfortunate circumstance.

But every once in a while the bearer of a bad hand will find
a way to beat the odds and cash all his chips in.

Seemingly victorious in the unfair game of life, if all was
lost could lightning strike the same place twice?

∽

I can still recall that day as if my memory had somehow been immune from the decay of time. It was an unusually hot and humid day on a weekend in early October of 1990. The first leaf had yet to fall and the initial frost of the oncoming winter, although close at hand, had not yet arrived. It was a lovely day to be outside our peach-colored house in our lower-class neighborhood on the north side of Omaha.

Our house was pretty run down, but it didn't stand out much because most houses in the area looked somewhat similar. It was a lively neighborhood, and everyone seemed to be outside enjoying the oddly warm fall day. I had no clue as to how that day would come to define my existence and, in essence, forever alter the course of my destiny.

My eleven-year-old sister, Tara, had rich caramel skin with gorgeous long dark hair and a knack for finding trouble. Although we both had different fathers, we never dared call each other half-brother or half-sister. We had always been extremely close. I suppose the fact that neither of our parents had any other children forced us to latch on to our mutual love for each other. Our mother and my sister's father had been divorced a few years before I was born. My own father indiscriminately had finally provided her with the love of a legitimate father figure; it was a love that she had forever longed in vain to discover in her own.

That day Tara was out with my cousins Bianca and Brett riding their bikes around the neighborhood. At the time I was unable to tag along, due to the fact that I had not yet been given a bicycle of my own. So instead, I was forced to be content with playing outside in front of the house. My mother was inside the house as usual and had her new boyfriend over.

Like many of my friends' parents, my parents had never been married although they had previously been engaged. The engagement recently had been called off. My parents also didn't live together, but still saw each other on a regular basis regarding me. My father had bought the house we lived in, and regardless of their relationship status he allowed my mother to continue to stay there with my sister and me.

Sometime around midafternoon, my father pulled up to the curb in front of the house in his 1983 brown Buick. I remember him storming into the house. I could hear him arguing with my mother from where I played. I was sure her new boyfriend who was visiting had something to do with it. My father was well known for sometimes being over the top with his jealousy.

He had asked my mother to take him back. She gave him back the engagement ring he had given her. She had already let go of a love that he still madly clutched onto. Heartbroken I presume, he gathered some of my clothes into a brown paper bag and then proceeded to put the bags into the rear seat of his car. He then sat me in the back seat next to my clothes, fastened my seatbelt, and closed the door. If he couldn't have her, it seemed he was intent on taking the only thing that he had left.

Still, somehow, I could sense that the drama was far from over. As I looked out the window, I could see both of my parents engaged in a heated argument with each other on our neighbor's lawn next door. My mother ran up to the car and pulled me from the backseat as the situation continued to escalate. Before I knew what was going on, I was being restrained by my mother's new boyfriend.

My mother ran inside the house and reemerged with a small handgun. She held the chrome twenty-two–caliber handgun by a pink handle, as it gleamed in the sunlight. She possessed the ignited desperation of a cornered mother bear protecting her precious cub.

At the same time, my sister arrived back at the house with my cousins, just in time to witness the situation as it continued to spiral out of control. Screaming, my sister jumped off her bike and ran into the house yelling, "I'm calling the police."

"Call them," my mother replied unyielding, almost as if she were an oblivious pawn of fate. As I looked around me, it seemed as if the entire neighborhood had congregated on the street to watch the drama unfold.

Some people say that throughout life we all have choices. And it is the choices that we alone make that determine our fate. Others believe that our lives are predetermined by some higher power, and that no matter what we do, we will arrive at whatever fate we are predestined to.

As I think back to that moment and envision all of those people failing to take action, I think I believe the latter. Something inside made me believe that bystander apathy wasn't solely responsible for letting what was about happen occur nonetheless. I have always believed that only fate could have made all those people watch so unengaged. Or maybe it brings us comfort to believe that when bad things happen for no reason at all, it must be part of some greater purpose over which we have no control.

Loathsome clouds had quietly been gathering over the situation for some time as a rapidly intensifying storm was brewing. As I was restrained in our front yard, I could see my parents in the middle of the street. My mother had pointed the gun at my father as he walked toward her. The first shot startled me like an unexpected lightning strike on a dark and thunderous night. The bullet had grazed his leg as he still approached her unwavering.

A hand unsuccessfully attempted to shield my eyes when suddenly I heard the dreadful strike of lightning for a second time. My father had been hit in the shoulder, but he still approached as if hardly affected. As I squirmed to get loose, I could see that my father had grabbed the gun and pointed it to his chest while my mother's finger still remained on the trigger. I noticed that he stood tall and steadfast, similar to a man who had already accepted his untimely end.

Yet the gaze in his eyes revealed thoughts of a person somewhat dumbfounded regarding the circumstances surrounding their final hour. I closed my eyes tight and heard lightning strike for the last time.

When the storm had finally passed over, I opened my eyes and saw my father's figure twisted on the concrete. He would be pronounced dead upon arrival at the hospital. His untimely passing would instantly create a martyr in the eyes of those who knew him best.

My mother walked away from the scene, as if still helplessly possessed by a power beyond her own comprehension. She picked me up while resting me on her hip and took me into the house.

"Why did you shoot Daddy" was all that I remember saying. I was four years old.

eac

In less than an instant my whole life changed. Although I was too young to realize it then, it was at that moment that my father's dream would become my own. We would soon share the dream of a Black child, thrown into a dark forest full of impossibilities, subsequently forced to choose between accepting an unfavorable reality and overcoming all obstacles to reemerge victorious.

I doubt I was ever prepared to take the torch but fate is never calculated. I never thought the game I would be forced to play was a fair one, but it was an opportunity to play the game nonetheless.

Growing up I would have a choice to make, either forever feel sorry for myself or take my destiny into my own hands. The day before I had been the son of an esquire, and in the blink of an eye I had become another statistic waiting to materialize. Unknowingly overwhelmed with an ambiance of déjà vu, the cycle of poverty had begun anew. My father's passing was like the violent death of a large star in calamitous clouds of supernova, and similar to the crushing gravity that condenses the remaining matter and creates a new sun in its place, the hopes of those around me created pressure equally dense, in anticipation that I too would become a star and shine just as bright.

Charles Darwin forever revolutionized science with his theory of evolution and belief that in our world only the physically fit survive. At an early age I didn't know much about Darwin, but my experiences would lead me to believe that regardless of how physically fit you are, if you aren't mentally strong, the world would eat you alive.

I never blamed my mother for what happened that day. I didn't think it was my place to judge. After all, hate couldn't change the past. She was all that I had left. At times I would blame myself instead, convinced that everything that had occurred had been my own fault. It was a long time before I stopped believing that had it not been for me my father would still be alive.

Eventually, I concluded that there was nothing anyone could have done. My life would come to revolve around the idea that I possessed the ability to actively stimulate change within my present and future, but there would never be anything I could do to change the past.

After only a few months in jail my mother would be released with a sentence of six years' probation. She became the first woman in Nebraska's history to receive such a light sentence involving a death during a domestic violence dispute. Just as her part in my nonfiction drama had seemingly concluded, she would return to an encore of melancholy as her role had not yet come to an end.

Regardless, I'm sure that whether she was guilty or not, having to look at me every day and remember what she was responsible for was more than enough punishment for anyone to bear. When she would return from prison, life would never be the same for any of us.

2

RISE OF THE P.H.O.E.N.I.X.

*Defying death the essence of a dream clutched onto
immortality, while emerging revitalized from the last
gasping breaths of fatality.*

*Stemming from a cradle tucked in the crease of paved streets,
springing forth anew it had survived the winter like the
last laugh of a fallen leaf.*

*From the depths of smoldering flames of cinnamon, myrrh,
and frankincense, it issued forth from the bowels of
antiquity a modern myth.*

*Similar to a prize-fighter whose destiny is to never be
defeated, so goes the story of the rise of the Phoenix.*

℘

T he day I had waited an eternity for had finally come. It was the hooding ceremony and commencement of my law school career. As I sat in the second row away from the stage in a purple and black robe, while brushing the swinging tassel from my view, the feelings that overwhelmed me were indescribable. I was fighting a fierce battle to hold back the tears. It was a battle in which I would prevail. I was going to uphold a promise to myself to stay strong all the way through the end.

As I sat next to my peers, we were all waiting to be called on to claim the fruits of our own labor. I didn't know what those next to me had done to obtain their degrees, but I had jumped through fire to get mine. As one of the few Blacks in a sea of faces, my thoughts strayed toward those who shared my socioeconomic background throughout America, who similarly were expected to excel on an uneven playing field while chasing dreams in boots made of steel.

Our row was soon called, and as I stood up, I peered out into the crowd. I saw the warm faces of those who had helped me throughout the years. On the road toward my destiny I had been sent angels to guide me at checkpoints along the way. While waiting in line to walk across the stage, I searched the crowd for my mother. Unable to find her, I thought of times when I had been younger and had vainly searched for a face that I often could never find. Then all of a sudden I could see her proud, beaming expression from across the auditorium.

I was proud of her that she had finally gotten rid of her demons, and for the first time in years had begun to let her true potential shine outward from within. I thought of all the times my mother and I had stood in line together, waiting to be saved by social welfare. I remembered how her disease had stolen all optimism. I knew my road here could have been a lot easier, but I had no regrets. In the end it had all made me stronger. This day wasn't just mine.

As thoughts bombarded my consciousness, I continued to take steps forward while the line progressed. I looked back into the crowd and met eyes with my sister as she gave a sincere smile. She had been alongside me dodging mortars of life's madness in the trenches of days far behind. There were many moments when her faith and reassurance had given me the edge to turn the tides of defeat.

I looked down at her hand grasping the handle of her cane, and she reminded me of a weathered warrior who had survived urban warfare. Although battered by worldly hazards, she had survived. She had survived when so many of her peers had fallen alongside her while attempting to navigate minefields of misfortune. As a former little Black girl who idolized my father as much as I did, this was her day just as much as it was mine.

The line slowly moved forward, and I could see my niece waving vigorously from the lap of my sister. I waved back and admired her beauty and innocence. By the time I had reached her tender age, my innocence had been long gone. I had sacrificed to ensure that she would never have to step into the dark forest that my father and I had emerged from. Today was her day.

I looked back into the crowd and scanned the room, and I could see my Aunt Mary Ann waving in the crowd. Although they were unrelated, I know that my father had been a big brother and a best friend to her. She had been in the front row when my father had climbed from poverty's pit to the peak of his achievements. She had taken me in like I was her own simply because she knew my father would have done the same. It had been her praises of my father that would motivate me to one day have others speak of me in the same light. I did my best to fill the void my father had left in her life. This was her day too.

As I inched forward ever closer to the stage, I had found my longtime mentor Maggie in the crowd. I instantly remembered the moment we had met, and she greeted me with her warm smile. I knew I wouldn't have made it had it not been for her seeing the potential within me. She had unlocked my talents and gave me the courage along with the direction to reach for the stars. She made me believe in the power of mentoring. This wouldn't be my day if it wasn't hers too.

When I had finally reached the stairway leading to the top of the stage, I waited impatiently on a set of stairs and pondered the fate of the children who had sat next to me on the steps of a concrete jungle. I thought about the number of times that my dreams were hanging in the balance. Today was mine.

The author (right) with longtime mentor and former Pro Pal Plus Mentoring Program Coordinator Maggie Kalkowski following law school graduation.

Unfortunately, I can't say that my dream was original. Yet, I can truly say that for the first time I was proud to be second. I stood on a stage that I had sacrificed everything to stand on. While waiting for my name to be called, I imagined my father next to me. I knew he was somewhere watching.

After hearing the moderator call out, "Ean Garrett," I stepped forward while leaving behind a past that I had sought so desperately to escape. I shook the hand of Supreme Court Justice Clarence Thomas, bracing myself for the possibility that at any time this moment would disappear, like a distant mirage in the midst of burning desert sands.

As I walked across the stage, I knew this was a ceremonial display that hard work pays. Through it all I was still alive, and although I took a few detours I had still arrived. And to my own disbelief like my father before me, I now knew what it felt like to touch a Juris Doctor degree. At the same time I now joined a small population of Blacks and growing population of Americans with advanced degrees. I finally felt truly free from the iron-clad shackles of poverty.

It was pure euphoria to see that a long shot in the dark had finally hit its mark. With the passing of my father, I had witnessed the death of a dream, and from day one it had been up to me to breathe life back into it. And so like the phoenix, a dream raised from my father's ashes, and for a second time a plot would be realized to escape from poverty, while becoming everything that statistical probabilities predicted I would never be.

For others it may have been a moderate accomplishment, but to those who had been alongside me in the midst of dark memories in the distant past, they understood the magnitude of the moment. I never imagined realizing my passions, but I was dogged to transform a fool's dream into something tangible that I could see, taste, and touch.

My accomplishments would come with a responsibility that from early on I had already accepted. It was my destiny to blaze a path out of the ghetto and return to lead the forgotten out of an urban wilderness and beyond the broken-promise land, to a place where dreams never die.

❦

To the hopeless and downtrodden, to every young boy and girl who ever went without or felt the burning sensation of defeat, resist the temptation to break. The architect lies within you to design your own destiny. At the dawn of a new decade, in a nation currently blanketed with uncertainty, a maturing generation comes of age while a new generation emerges. The emerging generation has the ability to put an end to the recurring cycles of poverty. Only with an open mind and hearts full of determination can we solidify our birthright that is commonly referred to as the American dream.

To the neglected and underprivileged, allow my words to serve as a compass to guide you when all hope disappears, and the end to all agony is seemingly far from near. In thoughts of optimism lie the hidden paths toward progression. The reality that you wake up to isn't the reality that you have to see or the one that has to be. Chase the things you want with the hunger of a starving man that yearns to eat, and never ever lie down with defeat.

My father and I shared a dream, which stemmed from the concept that regardless of one's uncontrollable circumstances, it is still possible to control your destiny. It is the liberation of the physical by the eradication of perceived limitations within one's own mind. These perceived limitations are merely learned in the form of societal norms and stereotypical assumptions. And like any rule these limitations can be destroyed altogether. The ability lies within us all not only to realize our full potential but to actualize it.

I wasn't the smartest, the most athletic, or the most talented, but I had a dream that gave my life purpose. Being far from perfect I had made multiple mistakes along the way. Yet, I refused to embrace what the world told me was possible while pursuing the seemingly impossible.

> "Yet, I refused to embrace what the world told me was possible while pursuing the seemingly impossible."

I just wanted to escape. I wanted to be more than the world expected of me as a Black male born in the world's greatest empire in history. I had to finish what my father once started. Now that his dream had been realized for a second time, it was my chance to start all over. It was a chance to chase my own passions and dream my own dreams. It was unbelievable to have played a part of such a remarkable story. Yet, as I stood at the finish line of the race toward my dreams, I could still vividly remember where it all began.

3

THE FORGOTTEN

On a hot summer day from an aerial view of the ghetto,

  young children found relief in an open fire hydrant's spray.

Olympic matches using self-taught gymnastics consisted of

  back flips in alleyways on dirty mattresses.

Pre-teens with futile hoops dreams and visions of the NBA,

  dunked on used tires nailed up in neighborhood driveways.

With feelings of being watched all play would cease, and

  looking up the police helicopter had nearly grazed the

  treetop leaves.

∽

A t a glance Omaha was a thriving metropolitan area in the heart of conservative America. Five Fortune 500 companies called the city home, along with a man who regularly competed for the title of the world's richest person, Warren Buffett. The mix of a progressive urban environment with the small-town atmosphere seemingly provided the perfect place to raise a family. But if you took a closer look, you would see that everything that glitters isn't gold.

It was a city cloaked in deceit, similar to a seemingly warm pair of outstretched hands that were in fact cold to the touch. The fact that the city was also home to some of the poorest Blacks in the country was routinely swept into a corner. That filthy corner was the north side of Omaha, and had become a cesspool for poverty. To date not much has changed: six in ten Black children still live in poverty.

North Omaha served as a microcosm, displaying the growing divide between the country's haves and have-nots. It was an area of the city that was wild and untamed, and it was the place I called home.

In Black America it is commonplace to glorify the ghetto. More than likely a movement to embrace what strangers to its environment have come to fear, reject, and label as undesirable. From my own perspective I didn't see anything glorious about where we stayed. Yet, for some reason there is something about that environment that one could only understand if you grew up there.

There is a shared connection that occurs when people struggle equally together. Eventually there develops a shared instinct for survival. Either you would live to tell about your account or the ghetto would consume you.

> "It was an area of the city that was wild and untamed, and it was the place I called home."

Our two-story house seemed to be as old as the earth itself. On the second floor the electricity didn't work, which was one thing my father had intended to fix before he passed away. There was also a hole in the roof that enticed all kinds of animal life, and during the day you could hear pigeons making random sounds in the attic. We also had roaches and mice, which at the time I didn't think was an issue, because unbelievably so many of our neighbors had bigger infestation problems.

But somehow even with all that being said, we got plenty of compliments from our neighbors that we had a nice home, which likely was because their living situation was often far worse.

My mother was short with a light complexion, dark curly hair, and a face full of freckles. She was permanently disabled from sickle cell anemia, a blood disease that is prominent in African Americans. Her sickness forced her to annually make frequent stays at local hospitals. During these times my sister and I would be taken in by other members of the family.

When she would return home, I would sit next to her as she slept and watch her as she was chained to her bed, not by iron links but by machines and plastic tubes feeding her medication to numb an eternal pain. It was pain from a disease for which there was no cure, and little effort had ever been made to find.

Because of her disease my mother had been unable to work, and like me she was already destined to become a casualty of statistical probabilities from an early age. Born into a family of ten children, my mother and her siblings had been taken away from my grandmother due to neglect around the time that my mother had barely begun to walk. After spending time in a juvenile detention center with her brothers and sisters, they would be split up and bounced around from foster home to foster home.

After her older foster parents had both passed away, she was on her own by age sixteen. Her own father, burdened with a number of other children, had not played much of an active role in her upbringing. He had been shot and killed by one of his mistresses in the middle of a feud involving another woman less than a few months after I was born. My mother was far from lazy and yearned to be a productive member of society, but her disease crippled any fair shot she had to actualize her innermost ambitions.

Although my parents were not together around the time my father passed, he had principally been our main source of income. Within the last few years leading up to his passing, his law firm had just begun to break away from that tough start-up phase of any small business. Yet his skills and passion had always shined in the courtroom, as opposed to balancing his budget sheets or hunting down his often impoverished clients. As a result, he had not yet elevated his small practice out of debt prior to his passing, and his creditors had devoured everything he had.

Prior to my father's untimely death my sister and I were well provided for. We would wake up on Christmas morning to a tree surrounded by gifts enough for multiple families. Like many parents it had been my father's dream to ensure that his children would side-step the disappointments he had experienced growing up, and in many ways he had succeeded. I had momentarily tasted some form of stability and all the promise that comes with it. Although we weren't wealthy and lived in a lower-class neighborhood, my father's presence still contributed greatly to my own well-being. Now that he was gone, our financial situation had become dismal.

My Aunt Trish moved in with us from Minneapolis to assist my mother while she was sick, and also to help raise us. She was short with a brown skin tone and a small frame, also sharing similar facial features with my mother, which is why many often confused the two. While growing up Aunt Trish and my mother had been inseparable and had even shared foster homes together. Like my mother she had endured the same life of obscurity and had never quite found the answers to all her problems. But without the extra help, we wouldn't have made it.

Like many other families in our neighborhood, we would come to depend solely on government assistance. My mother's income from her monthly disability checks amounted roughly to $11,000 a year, which at the time was well below the poverty line. We were the typical welfare family political pundits often bashed for unduly burdening society and not pulling their own weight. People often referred to my mother as the "welfare queen" because of her inclination toward shopping at local thrift stores or standing in line to receive food donations from neighborhood churches. With all the things she wasn't blessed with, she always had an unrivaled tenacity for survival, a shared characteristic that would later prove to be invaluable to me.

Our house was located on Twenty-Eighth and Laurel, in the heart of the Miller Park area. The area was notorious for gang violence, drug distribution, and prostitution. As I would come to find out, it was always easy to find trouble but anything productive was hard to come by. There were always plenty of kids who lived on my block, but most never stayed long, as their parents were either evicted or eventually sought out safer neighborhoods.

A boy named Adrian and I were the only kids who had been on the block for as long as I could remember. It wasn't hard for us to become the closest of friends. Adrian lived across the street in a white house with his parents and two sisters. His parents, like mine, had never been married but had been together for close to a decade. Adrian was a pretty hefty kid and was taunted about it every day as he frequently fought because of it.

During our early grade-school years, when we weren't fighting because of Adrian's weight, we were usually finding other ways to get into trouble. We would frequently break into abandoned houses in search of whatever treasures we could find. We often stole bikes or basketballs lying around in yards, along with other items from the neighborhood corner store. Our activities usually involved stealing things that we were too poor to afford. Neither of us had ever gotten into any real trouble but that would soon change.

Our neighborhood had become the battlefield of a gang war. The next block over on Twenty-Ninth Street, there was a gang called Deuce-nine. Deuce-nine was an oddity, as it was a gang comprised of two different gangs and integrated an unlikely combination of Crips and Bloods, which normally were bitter enemies. Usually a deadly mixture, old gang rivals had united, choosing a commonality in turf over differences in gang affiliation. It was common knowledge that you didn't walk on that block regardless of how much of an inconvenience it might be.

On the other side of the neighborhood was Camden block, a rival of Deuce-nine, and by living on Twenty-Eighth Street, we were caught right in the middle of an all-out war. It wasn't out of the ordinary to see a drive-by twice a week or so. Our street in particular had been shot up numerous times. Neighbors often told stories of bullets narrowly missing them while innocently spending an evening enjoying dinner at home. I often had nightmares that I was the victim of gun violence. Gun shots echoed in the streets as soon as the moon appeared in the night sky, and if you wanted to get any rest there was no alternative but to sleep through it.

Our dog barked throughout the night at drug enforcement agents staked out in our backyard trees. Wild foliage and untrimmed bushes had taken over our entire backyard. Without any kind of lamp posts or light fixtures in the rear of our home, it was a perfect place to covertly watch the crack house directly behind our own. After a drug bust we rarely heard our dog bark at night again. It was a quaint reminder of the desolate environment we were living in.

In such an environment any form of guidance in the right direction was our urban legend. Gang members were our only role models, and like a popular ghetto fraternity, everyone I knew was either in a gang or contemplating joining one. It was a way to find belonging, acceptance, and ironically safety. Those of us who weren't in gangs faced the prospect of having to deal with threats from every gang that we didn't belong to. Those who joined gangs were glorified, received a sense of belonging, and most importantly found protection. The fear of being the victim of gang violence was one that we all lived with and wanted more than anything to live without.

Gangs were a way to find guidance from older Black males—the sort of guidance that was impossible to find at home for the many of us who were fatherless. Eventually I had started not only to hang around, but to look up to those who were in gangs. Some gang members in particular, after taking a liking to me, had even taken me under their wing. There would soon come a time when my admiration for them would get me into trouble.

All over the neighborhood cap guns had become a local craze. Plenty of kids had them and every kid wanted one. Most likely, it was an unconscious attempt to imitate the violence that we had become so accustomed to. Since most children's parents wouldn't or couldn't afford to buy them, kids would steal them instead. I admit that I wanted one badly.

On a summer afternoon I decided to tag along with a group of older kids, many who happened to be gang affiliated. We were going to the local grocery store a couple miles away to steal cap guns. My mother, who was usually sick and bedridden, never had any clue as to the trouble I would often get into. Adrian had been too scared to come along, and his parents were strict to the point that he rarely was allowed to leave the neighborhood. It was a vain attempt by his parents to shield him from the grasp of the ghetto. I was nervous but readily seeking approval from my older peers.

As we entered the grocery store, I could tell that all of the attention was on us. As I look back at that moment, I could only imagine how we looked, five or six unsupervised Black juveniles walking around that grocery store. When we finally reached the toy aisle, a couple of my friends quickly grabbed a few cap guns, stuffed them under their shirts, and walked away slicker than the most veteran of thieves. I was now standing in the aisle alone, nervously peeking up at the security cameras.

I looked back at the cap guns and then glanced up at the security cameras again, and then toward each end of the aisle. After looking around for what I imagine was too long, I finally built up enough courage to grab the cap gun and stuff it inside my shirt. I immediately headed in the direction of the front door with none of my friends in sight. As I began to walk out of the store, I felt a hand grab me. It was the store security guard and I had been caught!

> "I had stereotypically begun to realize my full potential as another Black youth in the back of a police cruiser, headed down the road to nowhere."

As I sat in a dark room in a secluded part of the store for what seemed like ages, through the doorway I could see my friends looking from afar. I didn't want them to see that I had been crying, and I knew better than to tell on them. Soon afterward the police arrived and drove me home. I had been lucky that the grocery store had decided not to press any charges.

During the drive home I couldn't stop thinking about how disappointed my mother would be. Already, I had stereotypically begun to realize my full potential as another Black youth in the back of a police cruiser, headed down the road to nowhere. When I finally arrived on my street in the back of the police car, it seemed like everyone was outside, and they all were pointing in my direction whispering. I was embarrassed, and no words could describe the discipline my mother gave me that day. I was seven years old.

I knew I had messed up and I could tell that I was headed in the wrong direction. But it was hard to reject the love and acceptance that the neighborhood gave me for not telling on my friends, who had also stolen. Telling in any kind of way was the quickest way to lose friends, lose respect, and more importantly to get hurt. It was the first time that I would mess up, but by far it wouldn't be the last.

Regardless of the destructive behavior that I had begun to display, there were those who had not given up on me. Mr. Webster lived toward the end of our street and owned one of the nicest homes in the neighborhood. It was a white and black house with a newly paved driveway and the finest display of grass seen in any yard on the North side of Omaha. Although his house was still fairly modest, he made the most of it and kept it in immaculate condition.

Mr. Webster was a retired military veteran, and also a handsome older gentleman with a light complexion and full clean-kept silver hair. He lived with his older wife and teenage grandson. His grandson, nicknamed Animal, had made a notorious reputation for himself in the streets through the selling of drugs and his gang affiliation.

Whenever Animal was in jail, which was more often than not, Mr. Webster would employ me for a small wage to do work around his yard. I would push a lawnmower across his plush grass, pick up trash, trim bushes, or climb on top of a twenty-foot ladder to clean his gutters.

One Saturday morning in particular, I invited a group of friends to assist with my work load, having only the intent to put money in their pockets as well. As I introduced them to Mr. Webster, he gave me a timid look. He walked into his garage and brought back all the tools we would need. He then proceeded to walk back into the house, after explaining that he would be inside watching the Husker football game while we worked.

When the assigned tasks for the day had finally been completed, I had done almost all of the work alone, and my friends were nowhere to be found when Mr. Webster finally returned. Mr. Webster sat me down on the stairs outside of his house. He adamantly expressed his dislike of my friends. He called them lazy "riff raff," and doubted that they would amount to anything more. He went on to tell me that deep inside I was different.

I could tell that he felt guilty about being unable to save his grandson from the chaos of the ghetto. I'm sure the work he would regularly give me was more his second chance at redemption. It was a second chance to save another young soul from the same streets that had forever stolen the innocence of his grandson. After Mr. Webster had given me my day's pay, I walked home and curiously contemplated the meaning and the magnitude of his solemn words.

Our house was located a few blocks from the closest liquor store, one of the few Black-owned businesses in the ghetto. Every trip to the corner liquor store would become a perilous journey. Taking the shortest route we would pass through backyards avoiding rottweilers and pit bulls flashing mouthfuls of sharp and gnashing teeth. Because we lacked adequate healthcare, contracting rabies from a dog bite was our principal fear. But we would rather brave the back alleyways than risk becoming victims of poorly aimed bullets gone astray.

Standing in front of the store were drug feigns (addicts), the gang affiliated, and crack dealers gathered in communion. Inside the corner store liquor would line the walls. I could barely touch the top of the store counters as I struggled to reach the items I'd been sent to buy.

I exchanged a handwritten note and payment in change from my mother for a pack of Newport 100's from the store's owner. She knew my mother was often too sick to leave the confines of our home. Remembering that I had a single food stamp in my pocket, I placed the currency of those of us who knew the lifestyle of a lower class and spent it on chips that came in four twenty-five-cent bags. Taking my goods in a brown paper bag, I headed out into air that was constantly tense, as I prepared to make that treacherous journey home once again.

In the early 1990s, low-income housing projects were dotted throughout North Omaha. It was the city's feeble attempt to control drugs, prostitution, and crime by strategically placing the city's poor Blacks in designated locations. The most notorious of the housing projects were known as "Hill Top" and "Vietnam." Aunt Trish moved out for a while into the Vietnam projects, and often we would visit her for extended periods of time.

> "An island of poverty surrounded by an ocean of despair."

Named for an environment similar to that of a war zone, Vietnam was lawless. It was an island of poverty surrounded by an ocean of despair. While making the family drive to go and stay with Aunt Trish, riding into the projects eerily reminded me of the past. Turning down its narrow streets, I imagined what the Allied Forces must have felt like when they rode into Auschwitz and for the first time witnessed the casualties of human apathy.

While we were driving by, malnourished children would momentarily stop playing and stare back, like the last survivors of Nazi prison camps. While looking out of the car and peering at young victims of a broken system, I saw my own reflection in the car window and realized that they resembled me and I them. Like most victims of the Holocaust, it was unlikely that these children would ever live to see such desolate times come to an end. Naïve and unsuspecting, I had failed to conceptualize that my own odds of emancipation from the ghetto were just as grim.

The projects were surrounded by high gates, which seemed better equipped to keep things in as opposed to keeping things out. Toddlers and adolescents populated basketball courts scattered with drug needles, shattered bottles, and broken dreams. Gun shots routinely rang out in the early afternoon air, as commonly as the projects' few birds chirped while perched on the withering branches of rotting trees. The smell of death was pungent. I knew people died there often, and if you became too accustomed to living with death so near, sooner or later it would come for you.

But every once in a while, the ominous clouds would part over the Vietnam projects and the sun would shine through. To an average person driving by, the "Candy Man" probably appeared like nothing more than a homeless man who had stolen a bike. To the project youth he was Moses. He would ride into the projects on an old bicycle, while blaring the latest music from a boom-box taped to the back of his banana seat. Bearing gifts for children of the city's forgotten, while motivated by pure benevolence, he was routinely met with a reception fit for the coming of a Messiah.

As soon as we heard the music, all of the project children who were indoors and outside would run and chase the Candy Man. He would throw us every kind of sweet that you could ever imagine. For a moment, candy would line the streets and a diversity of color would momentarily paint an otherwise bleak canvas. Often the event transcended generations as uncles or grandmothers could be seen grabbing a jaw breaker or pocketing Tootsie Rolls.

> "I refused to be defined as nothing
> more than the lower-class grease
> and grime that lubricated the gears
> of a machine called America. "

Sitting on the project steps, devouring whatever sweets we had been nimble enough to catch, brought temporary relief from a harsh reality. At the time I couldn't have imagined, while eating from a box of Lemon Heads I had caught, that many of the children I sat next to would never escape the peril that was Vietnam. Even then my dreams unknowingly were precisely aligned with those of my father before me. I refused to be defined as nothing more than the lower-class grease and grime that lubricated the gears of a machine called America.

While others thought the American dream was an American facade and democracy nothing more than white hypocrisy, my elementary knowledge of our forefathers' concepts had led me to believe early on that they were on to something. I was sure destiny had more in store for me, but at that moment I just didn't know what or how it would be achieved—only if somehow I could take the entire projects with me. When we would leave Aunt Trish's, we were always glad to see the outside of those menacing gates, although we were ignorantly only trading the fire for the frying pan, the projects for the ghetto.

4

THE WHITE DEMON

*Each day tends to be more excruciating than the last, and
often beyond what one seemingly can bear.*

*Like magic, with one or two puffs all of their problems
instantly disappear.*

*Instead of carrying their burdens they chose to lay them to the
side, eagerly trading lows for artificial highs.*

*As those hopelessly addicted to a pipe or syringe, vigorously
and zealously begin to worship them;*

*They open up a sinister doorway to a false Eden, leading to
the home of the White Demon.*

I t's ironic how the words *white*, *pure*, and *liberating* are all used to describe something that undoubtedly possesses characteristics more fitting of a darker description. For many, crack or cocaine is some distant thing or fictitious evil that only exists on television or in the movies, but I was acquainted with it all too well.

How high-priced drugs such as cocaine arrived in our neighborhood from distant shores no one knew. Nonetheless drugs were abundant throughout my neighborhood, and although I'd rarely see any physically, I could easily see signs of their presence all around me.

It wasn't abnormal to hold a conversation with some of our older peers, most in their early teens, and momentarily be interrupted as they conducted a swift drug exchange with a neighborhood junky. Every once in a while, we saw one of those same older peers run past us as we played and hurdle a high fence, or dash through an alleyway. And as an overweight and out-of-shape police officer would struggle to pursue them, we would cheer them on as they narrowly escaped.

I took a liking to two brothers in particular who sold drugs. One was a thirteen-year-old "pretty boy" named Jermaine, who here and there sold crack and had chosen to be gang affiliated with the Bloods. He could be seen riding around the neighborhood on a chrome Dyno or GT, expensive trick bikes that were too costly for most kids' parents to afford and mostly owned by kids who sold drugs. Jermaine longed to imitate his older brother Deon who was fifteen.

Deon was gang affiliated as a Crip and sold crack more heavily than his younger brother Jermaine. One day while accompanying Deon as he made a few rounds, I gazed down at the sidewalk deep in thought. He looked me in my face and with a stern voice said, "Never look down. Always keep your head up."

With those words, he passed down one of the most important rules of survival in the ghetto. If I ever wanted to live to see an old age, I would have to constantly be aware of my surroundings. It was advice that I would never forget.

Every once in a while I'd witness Deon put his own advice into action as he was pursued by the police and dashed around a corner ditching a few rocks of crack. A watchful drug feign would always ensure that he'd never find them if he ever made it back.

I had also been heavily influenced by my older first cousin. At the early age of sixteen he already had a nice car, which was shiny red with speakers, rims, and neon lights underneath. Every time I saw him, I'd ask for a pair of sneakers or other nice apparel he was done wearing. His mother had been responsible for introducing him to the game of selling crack—the same drug she was addicted to. I tried to replicate his every move. It would take until he accidentally shot himself in the jaw while playing with his gun, along with the birth of his newborn son, for him to leave such a lifestyle lacking longevity behind. In later years, whenever I saw him occasionally, he would do his best to ensure that I never made the same mistakes or took a similar path.

Those who sold drugs were idolized for various reasons, especially by the ghetto's youth. Drug dealers, which often were gang members too, always had the nicest clothes and the most expensive cars, all things we longed for and desired. Selling drugs was a way to buy the things that we saw on television but could never afford. It was the quickest way to make money. A drug dealer could make in one day what he would make by working an honest forty-hour job for two weeks. The prospects of fast money made it hard to listen to our elders who preached about hard work and the importance of an education.

But the temptation for quick and easy money would be the downfall for many that I knew. At one point my sister had even been influenced by the selling and production of drugs. I walked into our upstairs bathroom and discovered my sister shaving soap into small pieces. The white shavings piled up along the side of the bathtub as she continued intent on her task. It wasn't uncommon for drug dealers to sell shaved soap in place of crack while tricking desperate drug addicts.

When I asked her what she was doing, she told me she intended to sell it. I didn't know what crack looked like back then, but I assumed that the shaved soap was pretty close. She never sold it directly but gave it to neighborhood drug dealers who, after selling it to a random crack addict in the neighborhood, would share the profits with her.

Around the same time gang violence throughout the neighborhood had climaxed. A boy named Arthur from the gang Deuce-nine had been killed in a drive-by on the next block over from mine. Arthur had been well liked by many, so a speedy retaliation was expected. For some reason there was a rumor going around that my sister had something to do with Arthur's death. There were threats upon her life, and it was no longer safe for her to live with us anymore. In addition she also had been performing poorly during her first year of high school and had failed every single one of her classes.

Her biological father lived in Detroit where she had been born, and it was decided that it would be in her best interest to move back with him. The day she finally left I wept. When she moved to Detroit, it was difficult to cope. After my father's death she had been mostly all that I could rely on. Now I was alone, and things would continue to spiral out of control.

There had been talk throughout the neighborhood that my Aunt Trish and my mom were using drugs. One of my friends told me that they had overheard their parents talking about it. Initially, I didn't believe them, and I didn't want to believe them. For some reason, I had assumed that my aunt could be doing drugs but never my own mother. It soon became obvious that I was wrong.

The rumors coincided with a string of burglaries where our house had been broken into and all of our belongings had been taken. For a long time, I had assumed that everything that had been going wrong in our house had been solely because of the bad neighborhood that we lived in. It wasn't until a little later that I started to piece everything together.

When Aunt Trish and her boyfriend would get into fights or split up, she would come and stay with us. On a school night, I observed her sleeping on top of a blanket on the floor of the living room with a strange man whom I had never seen before. She always had random guests, so I didn't think much of it.

When I woke up the next morning, she had numerous scratches and scrapes all over her body. Our television was gone. The strange man whom she had been sleeping with the night before had taken our television. My aunt had jumped on top of his car in an effort to recover the stolen property and had fallen off. As a result she had been scraped up severely. It was a common occurrence for those addicted to drugs to steal others' belongings to later sell in an attempt to temporarily satisfy their addictions.

After a while I was tired of fighting with kids who would tell me that my mother was on drugs. I called my sister to vent and she confirmed that the rumors were true. She had caught my mother smoking crack previously but had never told me.

I couldn't believe it. At my young age I only knew that crack had a negative stigma attached to it. I had yet to discover just how harmful the drug could be. The depression dealing with my father's death had overcome her, and my Aunt Trish's boyfriend introduced her to the best form of relief that he knew of.

As my mother's addiction became worse, so did the amount of traffic that came in and out of our house. Most of them were men who sold drugs to my aunt or my mother. Others had come to buy pain pills that my mother took for her sickle cell and also sold for extra money. Since sickle cell had no cure, all her doctors could do was give her prescription medication to relieve the pain. Many of the medications she took were level-one narcotics, such as Dilaudid, morphine, or Demerol. On the street, she could easily get thirty dollars for one pill, if not more. But unfortunately, I would come to find out that selling pills wasn't the only thing she did for extra money.

It was late when the front door opened and my mother let a young man into the house. He looked as if he couldn't have been any older than his early twenties. When he walked into the living room, I could feel the atmosphere in the house change. As they both walked upstairs, he made a sexual gesture behind her back and looked in my direction with a smile as he did so.

I couldn't see his face very well because the television was the only light, and I was still half asleep on the living room sofa. The glare from the television cast a white glow across his face as I sank under the covers in the dim light and pretended to still be asleep. As he stuck his tongue out, I imagined a forked tongue extending from the head of a white serpent. I knew that they were both possessed by forces far beyond the comprehension of their clouded minds.

The air was filled with muffled noises of the unthinkable. I tried to sleep through it pretending that it was all a bad dream. I closed my eyes tight and imagined being in another place, anyplace except in that moment. After what seemed like an eternity they both returned from upstairs, and he had a devilish grin on his face.

At the time the drugs were more important to her than her own well-being, so I guess I shouldn't have been surprised she wasn't considering me. I tried to remember that what she had become wasn't who she really was or the person she was destined to be.

On my mother's side of the family, she and my Aunt Trish weren't the only ones who had issues with drug addiction, or the addiction to the quick and easy money that selling drugs could provide. A good portion of my family at some point had either been addicted to drugs or sold them. Most members of our family who I knew that had money all sold drugs. I had an uncle in particular who had made a name for himself selling crack. I remember how he would arrive on our block and stop in front of our house in a blue Mercedes-Benz with shiny rims, one of four cars that he owned.

Although I didn't see my uncle often, I always looked forward to seeing him, because he would always give me money anytime he saw me. But selling drugs tends

to be a fast life, and if you're successful at all, you begin
to attract a lot of negative attention. Not long after I
had last seen him, he was shot and killed as he opened
his front door. Thought to be drug related, his murder
remains unsolved to this day.

> "The feeling that overtook me every time
> the White Demon walked in my front door
> and sucked the soul out of my family was
> my primary deterrent."

His funeral would be the first that I ever attended.
When my father passed, for some reason neither my
sister nor I had been in attendance. During my uncle's
funeral I remember long, dark, and sad faces draped in
deep shades of black. From early on I witnessed the evil
that drugs were capable of, and as I walked up to his
casket and looked into his pale lifeless face, I thought
that there had to be another way to make it.

Many often asked why I never sold crack or cocaine
like so many others that I had known. I think there is
no single explanation. I believe that more than anything
the feeling that overtook me every time the White
Demon walked in my front door and sucked the soul
out of my family was my primary deterrent. There was
just no way that I could take part in the destruction
of entire families, communities, and my own race for a
small profit. They were profits that I thought were mere
bread crumbs in the grand scheme of the economic

picture. Although when one is starving, bread crumbs can be the difference between life and death.

Although I never directly participated or promoted the selling of crack or cocaine, I always had empathy for those who did. I understood why young Black men could be drawn into selling drugs in an effort to extract themselves from the clutches of poverty. It was an instant solution to the prospects of a desperate life within the confines of the ghetto. Yet, I knew that there had to be more than what had been readily available to me, and I felt I deserved more than what was in front me.

Most people I knew who sold drugs did so as a desperate means to make a living, when otherwise it would have been difficult to do so. Adolescent mistakes would give misguided youth early criminal records, making it difficult to later find any gainful employment, which would result in a relapse to the game of selling drugs. In contrast, those who merely used drugs did so to temporarily escape poverty or other types of despair.

I could tell that my mother was taking drugs to escape from her own reality and the death of my father. But at that point I had made up my mind that by taking drugs she was being selfish and couldn't see how her actions were affecting me and my sister. You never know how the things that you do affect the people around you, and most importantly the ones you love.

Some say it exists where children play behind a white picket
   fence, and decorated Christmas trees grow that Santa
   Claus will never miss.

A fabled place where normalcy sleeps tucked in so safe and
   sound, also providing the perfect platform to blast off
   straight into the clouds.

It is a blissful target unlikely ever to be found, while taking
   aim strapped to realities stifling merry go-round

In the turmoil of each turn the screams of the forgotten are
   drowned, as they pray for an evasive calm to befall their
   turbulent playground.

Afterter graduating from the fourth grade at Miller Park Elementary School, every kid in our neighborhood attended Sherman Elementary School for the fifth and sixth grades. It was a school oddly placed miles away near Omaha's local airport. The student body primarily was comprised of poor Blacks and whites from the surrounding area. All stemming from the same demographic we each possessed more commonalities than differences. Before extrinsic forces taught us the value of our skin tones, we were all boiling in the same pot. They too were forgotten.

Although we were all temporarily removed from our environment while in school, aspects of the ghetto ran through our veins. I fought in the hallways exchanging jabs and punches with my peers while honing our survival skills. By exhibiting any signs of weakness one would instantly be subjected to harassment and physical assault. A visit to the principal's office was merely an acceptable consequence to earning the respect necessary to be left alone.

Regardless of everything going on inside and outside of the classroom, I tried my best to stay focused. I knew that school was important and I treated it so. If I missed the bus, although it was miles away, I walked to school anyway. My mother didn't have a car at the time, so if I was going to make it to school after missing the bus, the shoes on my feet would have to get me there.

While attending Sherman Elementary I performed extremely well and was even recommended to skip from the fifth to the sixth grade. After noticing my performance, my English teacher gave me a two-hundred-fifty-page book to read in order to test my reading comprehension. I read the book in less than a day.

My teacher didn't believe that I had read the book so quickly and as a result gave me an exam on the material. I only missed one question on the test. But my opportunity to excel would soon come to an end. We were moving out of the neighborhood, and I would have to switch schools.

> "I would be forced to trade
> opportunity for instability."

The house we lived in, which my father had bought, was in my name after his death. As a result of my mother's inability to come up with the money to pay the taxes on the property, we were evicted. Once again, like at many points in my then unforeseen future, I would be forced to trade opportunity for instability.

Shortly before we moved out of the neighborhood, I had become more involved in gang-related activity. I went through the initial stages of becoming gang affiliated and fought a group of younger gang members in order to gain the respect necessary to become a part of the neighborhood gang Deuce-nine.

At the time it seemed like the natural thing to do. After all, I was following the ones that I looked up to. Without the means to travel outside your immediate surroundings, or to become exposed to something more, it tends to be hard to gain any type any insight to what else is out there that you might seek to obtain. I was headed down a path of ruin. Looking back, I am sure that losing our home was a blessing in disguise.

Around the time that we had lost our house, my mother had been dating a man named Mr. Blake. They had been dating on and off since I was seven years old. When they had first begun to date, their relationship was extremely limited in scope. My mother would entertain him in an effort to receive financial assistance and support. He was a slightly overweight man and was no less than fifty years old, but he had always been very kind to me.

After we were evicted, my mother and I stayed with Mr. Blake in a small two-bedroom apartment, and their relationship eventually became more. His older children, mostly in their thirties, would often stay with him. Some would make regular stays between serving prison sentences which varied in length. One had even gained notoriety as a serial bank robber.

Because of the lack of space, my mother and I often were forced to sleep in the same bed, while one of Mr. Blake's children occupied the second bedroom and he slept on the couch. Although he also had an infestation problem, while living with Mr. Blake there was always food and the bills were always paid. I knew our situation could have been worse, and as a result I tried to make the most of it. I couldn't afford to let it deter me.

After the move I attended Field Club Elementary for the fifth and sixth grades. I had trouble adjusting to my new school. With the demographics of my previous school, the only whites that I had known were those whose trailer homes I would often walk past on my way to school whenever I missed the bus, or those who inhabited our neighborhood and occupied our same economic position. My new school was dead center in the middle of a well-to-do neighborhood and was attended mostly by middle- to upper-middle-class whites.

Initially, I was grossly underprepared for the harder curriculum, which may have been the result of my prior elementary school having some of the lowest standardized test scores in the city. Eventually, I would begin to perform at a level that I had been previously accustomed to.

It was during this short period of my life that for the first time I realized that I was poor. I often fought because my classmates made fun of the clothes I wore. Most of my clothes were handed down from my older cousins, and it wasn't out of the ordinary for some of them to have holes in them. It was evident based on the way I talked and the way I dressed that I was different. I hated my new school, and I wished that we had never moved in the first place.

It was around this time that the lack of a father figure also began to take a toll on me. In my previous neighborhood most parents were rarely heavily involved in their children's schooling, so when I came alone to a parent-teacher conference, it wasn't out of the ordinary. My own mother, with her disability and drug addiction, rarely came to support me during school-related activities.

> "The vast majority of kids that I knew from my previous neighborhood either never knew their father, knew him and hated him, knew when he would be released from prison, or knew where he was buried."

At my current majority white school, parents were deeply involved and dedicated to ensuring their children's success, and for the first time I was exposed to active father figures all around me. When I lived in the ghetto, being fatherless didn't affect me to the same extent, because most kids were fatherless. The vast majority of kids that I knew from my previous neighborhood either never knew their father, knew him and hated him, knew when he would be released from prison, or knew where he was buried.

Every once in a while my friends and I would discuss how we regretted not having father figures, especially my friends who were Black males. Our circumstances confined us in a zoo, where our race and gender placed us on a list of endangered species that society would conduct countless studies on to determine why we had taken a turn for the worst.

Fathers serve as living time capsules full of their own past experiences and those of their fathers before them. They have life-learned lessons of successes and failures to pass on to the next generation, in order for the next generation to build and improve upon what their fathers taught them. Like many other young Black males that I knew who were fatherless, I was forced to navigate through life in the dark, and like the blind the lack of sight subsequently often becomes disabling. If I was going to make it, I'd have to learn to survive without a father.

Although we moved out of my old neighborhood, we still lived in a low-income apartment complex that was surrounded by a lower-middle-class neighborhood. There weren't many kids in Mr. Blake's apartment complex, but eventually I made a few friends in the surrounding neighborhood. In particular I became friends with a white kid named Zach, and I would often hang with his older brothers and him.

Regardless of the fact that they were seemingly from lower-middle-class households, my new friends were not completely different from the old friends I had left behind. In fact, they would turn out to be just as bad an influence. They already had the habit of smoking cigarettes and were pretty young with the oldest being in junior high school. I had no idea who was buying them cigarettes at such a young age, but eventually peer pressure began to take its toll on me, and before long I tried smoking too.

I was just trying to fit in although I'm sure I looked ridiculous coughing profusely. I doubt I even knew how to inhale. Ultimately, I remember being turned off by how they would argue with each other over who was more addicted, and after less than a week I quit. But before I could get into any more trouble, we suddenly moved again.

This time we were staying downtown in a newly renovated apartment, compliments of the section eight public housing program. This would be the first time that I would live without roaches or mice and had hoped that I'd never have to see any again. Luckily we didn't move too far away from my school and as a result I didn't have to switch schools when we moved. Things seemed to somewhat be taking a turn for the better.

Although the apartment was nice and my immediate neighborhood seemed better, there were still some aspects that had failed to change. On my way to elementary school as the first rays of sun were chasing down the few remaining patches of midnight blue and violet, I passed prostitutes as they exited foreign cars fresh from overnight stays. I avoided the homeless as they huddled in dry places next to the sidewalk sleeping with everything they owned.

Walking onto the curb after crossing the street I walked in the shadow of an abandoned building that resembled an early twentieth-century brothel. Next to the building sat a dumpster that I would discard trash into from time to time. It was the same dumpster that a dead body been discovered in recently. Neighbors quickly walked past as if purposefully forgetting such a quaint reminder of our collective circumstance.

This part of town was a lot more diverse than what I was used to. There were a few Blacks, but mostly whites and Hispanics lived in my neighborhood. I would come to be friends with them all, but somehow I always befriended trouble.

Chad was a lanky white kid with dirty blonde hair. He lived next door to my apartment complex with his mother and two older brothers. He also smoked cigarettes but I had enough of those from my previous experience. It was natural for us to become friends because of how close we lived to each other. With not too many kids in the surrounding area there wasn't much to do, which made it easy for us to get into trouble.

At the time I was only in the sixth grade and Chad was a freshman at the neighborhood high school. One evening he invited me to walk down to the high school, which was less than a mile away, so I didn't mind. Upon arriving, I discovered that the high school was closed for the day, but Chad seemed to have expected this. After walking around the high school we discovered an open window.

First, Chad climbed in the window and then he helped me inside. The aged floor boards creaked under our feet as we climbed down from the window sill. We walked down the dark hallway and entered a room that appeared to be the high school bookstore.

Chad went straight for the safe while I wandered around and grabbed a pair of shorts and a water bottle. After we safely made off with the stolen goods, Chad would later be discovered by school officials and expelled due to bragging to his fellow classmates about the incident.

Somehow we managed to stay in the new apartment for barely a year before we were evicted. Although my mother was usually home physically, mentally she had escaped and refused to come back. After being evicted we moved back in with Mr. Blake, and my mother continued to battle with her drug addiction. This time my mom would stay a lot longer, but I couldn't say the same for myself.

Just as I had begun junior high I started getting into more and more arguments with my mother. She had been in and out of rehab and had failed to clean herself up. One day our verbal argument became physical. As I looked up from the ground after being freshly knocked down, I knew the woman hovering above me wasn't my mother.

It wasn't hard to realize that it was time for me to leave. I loved her but at that time she needed to love herself first before she could adequately love me in return. That very same night I took enough clothes for the next day of school and went to stay with my Uncle George.

Uncle George, who was named after my grandfather, was my dad's only full-blood sibling. He was extremely short, had a brown complexion, was bald, and as stern as they came. He also was a pastor of his own church, which would be a huge change for me. I actually didn't know him that well either. After the death of my father he never came around very often. When I first moved in, his second wife and stepson were also staying with him, neither of whom I would get along with.

Within a week, I came back to get all of my belongings from Mr. Blake's apartment. I could tell Mr. Blake and my mother were surprised I was actually moving out. But I was tired of staying there and I needed a change. My uncle's house was clean and provided a sense of stability. The only thing that I wouldn't be used to was the abundance of strict rules that I would now be required to adhere to.

Uncle George lived in a fairly bad neighborhood, and we were seldom allowed to travel far from the house. While staying with my uncle I attended church four times a week, which I admit definitely had a good influence on me. I remember that I had not been staying there long before he gave me a crimson-colored bible with my name embroidered in gold on the front cover. It would be the most valuable gift I had ever been given.

Before long I began to have issues with my uncle at home. I thought my uncle's behavior was eerily reminiscent of the way my grandfather had treated him and my father during their youth. We also got into verbal confrontations over things that I thought were small. It wasn't a secret that he and my father had a bitter sibling rivalry, and I felt that it was possible that he saw a little too much of my father in me.

> "Life had slowly become a game of musical chairs, and as the music played, I traveled from place to place."

I loved my uncle and stayed there for as long as I could stand to be there, but before long the situation had failed to work out and I would end up moving again. Life had slowly become a game of musical chairs, and as the music played, I traveled from place to place attempting to discover the winning situation to settle down in. I had begun to run out of options as my alternatives increasingly dwindled. I was intent on ensuring that regardless of everything around me, as soon as the pandemonium had come to an end, I would still remain standing steadfast enduring through it all.

6

MENTORING OPENS DOORS

Confined to dark places a seed struggles to grow, and without
light to feed its potential its full bloom will never show.

Lacking stable roots the slightest rain sweeps it down stream,
while also washing away the future of which it once
dreamed.

It is similar to a map without a compass rose, or a starless
night to a sailor navigating waters unknown.

Its last hope is a helping hand to guide it back to land, and
provide it with the tools for endless growth to begin.

Mentoring at its core is the selfless commitment to transfer useful knowledge to future generations so that they may prosper through its successful application. The sharing of valuable information has been the key to human progress throughout history.

In antiquity, the Greek philosopher Socrates mentored Plato, passing on coveted knowledge in developing areas such as biology, physics, and astronomy. Plato went on to mentor Aristotle, who in turn mentored the ancient king of Macedonia, Alexander the Great. As knowledge was passed on, ideas and philosophies became more developed and refined. Each subsequent generation possessed more tools than the last to assist in the achievement of their ultimate goals.

Today, mentoring is commonly thought of in terms of a more privileged individual providing guidance and support to an unfortunate young person. This narrow view is often misleading. The potential in mentoring is much more far-reaching. Through a small consistent investment in time, a mentor can change a life, and in turn that life can change the world. I personally had yet to discover just how powerful mentoring would be.

During middle school I had academically been performing fairly well. Thanks partly to the relatively increased stability that my uncle's home had provided, I had finally been given the ability to focus primarily on school. Yet, without an adequate role model or a constant and engaged figure in my life, the void left by the absence of my father became a constantly expanding depression in the landscape of my consciousness. Although consumed with the obsessive thoughts of a dream, I still lacked the guidance to assist me in actualizing it. But that would soon all change.

> "The void left by the absence of my father became a constantly expanding depression in the landscape of my consciousness."

It was a regular school day and the hallways at my middle school were empty, with the exception of a few loiterers abusing bathroom privileges. It was a couple hours past noon when I walked into the counselor's office. I had no idea what I was being called down for, but was happy to be getting out of class nonetheless.

After waiting for what seemed like forever, another student finally emerged from a room, and I was directed inside and told to take a seat at a table with two chairs across from each other. On the other side of the table stood a short, vibrant, and seemingly personable woman wearing the most sincere smile with her hand warmly extended to greet me.

The meeting was an interview in order to become a participant in a mentoring program at a local community college. It was my guess that some teacher, counselor, or administrator had recommended me. The woman's name was Maggie Kalkowski. She was a middle-aged white woman who was the coordinator of the mentoring program and later would prove to be genuine in her quest to help underprivileged youth. My interview had been impressive enough to land me a spot in the program.

The mentoring program was called Pro Pal Plus. Fundamentally the program was brilliant. The program took junior high and high school students and matched them with a mentor, while simultaneously providing them with essential job and life skills. Program participants were also given a fair amount of money to use for legitimate purposes upon graduation from high school and the program.

Mentoring activities could consist of a mentee enjoying dinner with a mentor's family or attending a baseball game. At times mentors would even serve as a personal life coach. More than anything having a mentor was simply the extra support that would serve as a catalyst for positive change in the life of an at-risk youth.

Overall, the commitment required of mentors was slight compared to the benefits to those of us who received mentoring. Just knowing that an extra hand was there when needed made all the difference, but at the time mentoring was the last thing on my mind.

After moving out of my uncle's house, I would stay with a close cousin of mine named Bianca. She was the daughter of my Aunt Mary Ann. Bianca had an almond complexion, was slightly overweight, and had a flawless smile with full cheeks. She was about six years older than I, and although we had been somewhat distant while young, the years had brought us closer together. She had even been there to witness the passing of my father.

Bianca stayed in an old apartment complex that was similar to Mr. Blake's, in that it was a poor and run-down development in the midst of a middle-class area. She had been kind enough to allow me to sleep in her room. I spent my nights on a mattress on the floor while she slept in her living room on a futon. I rarely went outside and would leave with friends whenever I wasn't at the apartment doing homework. I was thankful not to be at my uncle's house or Mr. Blake's, and was appreciative that Bianca had given me a place to stay.

My mom was fresh out of rehab and supposedly was doing well. Eventually, Mr. Blake talked me into staying with her again. This time she stayed in a brand new section eight apartment unit in Northwest Omaha. In my experience, section eight housing was a poor alternative to massive project development complexes, which were promoted by the city's recent reverse gentrification trend, in which whites were increasingly moving from the suburbs to the inner city.

Omaha had made an effort within the past few years to destroy all the housing projects in North Omaha including Vietnam, and as a result the city's poor were dispersed into different pockets throughout the city. Section eight was successful in moving the problem, but hardly victorious in solving it as I would soon discover.

In our new apartment building there were plenty of kids to keep me entertained, but many of the same negative aspects of my prior environments had reemerged. I often fought with neighborhood kids in the hallways of our building. Our apartment located on the first floor of the complex had also been broken into. Although I had moved out of the heart of the ghetto I had yet to flee far enough.

"Section eight was successful in moving the problem, but hardly victorious in solving it."

I had failed to create any meaningful friendships while living there with one exception. Ricky was fairly tall for his age, wore his hair braided back, had a light complexion, and a magnetic personality. We lived in the same hallway of the apartment complex, so it became only natural for us to become close friends.

He lived with his grandmother along with his two younger brothers. Looking no more than nineteen years of age, he had never finished high school, smoked marijuana often, and also sold it. He respected the fact that I didn't smoke, and I respected him likewise that he never pressured me to.

Usually our activities solely consisted of grabbing a basketball and heading down to Orchard Park, the neighborhood basketball court. I thought he was cool, and I admired him in many ways excluding his lifestyle involving the use and sale of drugs. He also was gang affiliated and extremely vocal about it, behavior which I had become comfortably accustomed to involving my friendships and experiences in the past. I considered him the only real friend that I had during such volatile times.

I never knew why he had dropped out of school or why his grandmother supported both his brothers and himself as opposed to his parents. In contrast, I'm sure it was obvious that a similar secrecy was imbedded all over my daily expression, but like many who learn to carry the accumulated burdens of misfortune, neither of us ever mentioned it. We shared an invisible connection stemming from the experience of navigating the maze of a similar struggle.

It was clear that Ricky had accepted his situation and couldn't imagine that he would ever be more than what he was. I wish I could tell you that he was wrong, but every story doesn't have a happy ending. Not many years later, I would learn that he would die in prison from causes unknown. His life mirrored the repetitive cycle of the stereotypical young Black male in America. The essence of my dream revolved around that idea that I would do whatever it took to ensure that my fate would be different.

Around this time I was getting ready to start high school and was in dire need of some form of stability. This would be a pivotal point in my quest to realize the shared dreams of my father. I knew that I would have to perform well in high school in order to go to college. If college could free me from my current situation, then it was a place that I was determined to get to. But there were more immediate issues that would take priority on my mental list of things to do.

> "If college could free me from my current situation, then it was a place that I was determined to get to."

Now that I had turned fourteen I was old enough to work so that I could buy my own things. I had become tired of people making fun of the clothes I wore and was sound in my quest to avoid the criticisms of my peers. I caught three buses to work at a movie theater located about ten miles away across town. At the age of fifteen it was one of the few places that I could work. I didn't make much money, but I was determined to become self-sufficient and proactive in altering my current situation.

During my freshmen year of high school I had been lucky enough to get into Central High School. It was plagued with the same issues that most public inner city high schools faced around the country. Unruly teens fought frequently in the hallways in between classes or during the lunch hour. A group of my young Black male peers could be seen after school gambling, while discreetly rolling dice and playing craps underneath the stairs leading to the second floor.

One day during my first semester of my freshman year before gym class, as I sat next to my locker mate, I laced up my gym shoes as he began to change into our mandatory gym uniform. He had an olive complexion, always wore expensive urban clothing or sneakers, and reminded me of every friend I had who had ever sold drugs. As I was busy placing a few articles of clothing in the bottom of my locker, my locker mate took a black nine millimeter gun from his waistband and placed it underneath my clothes.

He asked me not to say anything to anyone about it. School officials often had warned us that if this situation were to occur to notify them immediately. But the school officials didn't live in the same world I did, a world where it was normal to see a gun and abnormal to tell on those who broke rules or scoffed at the idea of authority figures.

Nonetheless, I could easily imagine what life he was living and why he needed to bring a gun to school. Regardless of what type of lifestyle he had come to live, it was one I didn't want any part of if I had to carry a gun everywhere I went. After lacing my shoe strings tight, I looked back up in his direction and promised I wouldn't say anything.

Although Central High had its shortcomings it was still the best public high school in the city and was prominent for its strong academics and rich heritage. When Nebraska and the surrounding states had been western territories prior to statehood, the high school had served as the territorial capitol building. Above all it was a college preparatory school, and college was exactly where I intended to go.

My mother seemed to be doing fine for a month or two before she went right back to her old vices. I tried my best to keep it from distracting me, but my effort was in vain. I never actually saw her smoke crack, but I still knew she was doing it. Drug dealers would still come over on a regular basis to sell it to her, and she would stay in the bathroom all day with the door locked. It wasn't long before my school work began to suffer.

School was my escape from the chaos at home, although it had failed to provide much of a relief. My first semester of high school I had been enrolled in all honors courses. By the end of my first semester of high school I was failing in almost all of them.

Every once in a blue moon my mother would come to pick me up from school. A messenger would deliver a note to my teacher during a class lecture. My teacher would call my name out loud in front of the classroom. After grabbing my belongings I would grab the note and head to the main office.

Walking into the high school's main office, I would always find my mother patiently waiting with a meager smile. Her hair would be untidy underneath a skull cap prematurely weathered by turbulent times. Her clothing gave the impression that she cared little for her appearance.

While walking down the busy hallways with my mother, I couldn't help but feel embarrassed about how she looked. Even while filled with a sense of embarrassment, I was ready to fight the first person to snicker or make sly remarks about her appearance. Regardless of how she appeared on the outside I always put her on the highest pedestal. I remembered the beauty that lay beneath her disorderly attire. At the time she was the only parent that I had left, so I embraced her nonetheless.

Christmas at the new apartment would also prove to be one of my most humbling experiences. After my father passed away, I was happy to get one gift. This Christmas morning, I would wake up to a bare tree with nothing but lonely pine needles underneath. It was sign of how out of control my mother's drug addiction had become.

Around that time my sister moved back in town from Detroit, and I was grateful when she decided to move in with us. My mother and sister immediately didn't get along, and my sister moved out as quickly as she had moved in. Once my sister had her own place, I saw my chance to escape and decided to move in with her.

Staying with my sister was beneficial in a number of ways. She kept a clean house and always kept food in the refrigerator. It also didn't hurt that she lived within walking distance of my high school. It was a relief to once again taste stability.

My sister had graduated from high school a few years earlier and was now working as a certified nursing assistant at various nursing homes throughout the city. One thing she did was provide me with an example of hard work as she was constantly working double shifts to support us. But with an hourly wage of nine dollars, she didn't have a choice. It was then that I refused to live day to day or check to check. I saw how much she was stressed out every single day. I made up my mind then that my life would be different.

In the midst of everything, I participated in my mentoring program regularly. My mother and sister thought having a mentor would be beneficial for me, and they welcomed any help in guiding me in the right direction. The program had been unsuccessful in matching me with a mentor and the coordinator Maggie ended up filling that role.

The program taught us useful skills, including tasks as simple as endorsing a check, to things as intricate as proposing a business plan. Probably the most beneficial aspect of the program was the fact that it allowed us to travel and become exposed to various experiences outside our city. Trips outside of the city primarily involved college tours mixed with sightseeing. All of the kids in the program fit into the same underprivileged demographic.

Most of us never would have had the opportunity to travel or otherwise be exposed to the opportunities involved with the program. More than anything I wanted to make it out of my situation, and I saw the program as a way to take me far. Only I never could have imagined how far it would take me.

It was the morning of September 11, 2001, and my sophomore year of high school had just begun. This was only the second time I had ever been on a plane before. Mollie, who was a fellow participant in my mentoring program, was sitting next to Maggie, and both seemed to be sleeping like exhausted children. On the other hand I was wide awake.

I couldn't stop going over my speech in my head time and time again. I had never spoken in front of a crowd before and was somewhat nervous at the prospect. Yet, I completely looked forward to the opportunity nonetheless.

After less than an hour into the flight we started to descend. I could sense confusion coming from the passengers all around me. Our flight was supposed to be non-stop to Washington, D.C. Mollie and I were scheduled to introduce then-Nebraska Congressman and legendary Nebraska football coach Tom Osborne at an award ceremony later that afternoon, which would honor his work in mentoring.

MENTOR, which was my mentoring program's umbrella organization, was hosting the event and had asked us to participate. We had even made our local newspaper for attending the event. Finally, the plane arrived at the gate and the captain told us we had landed in Minneapolis. Everyone was instructed to gather their things and exit the plane with no inclination as to why.

After exiting the plane and entering the terminal slightly confused, we saw a crowd congregating in a coffee shop nearby. When we walked over to see if we could find out any information, everyone was hovering around the television. Looking around I observed a woman with her make-up smeared from tears. As I looked at the television for myself I could see why we had been grounded.

A plane had flown into one of the World Trade Center towers while we had been in the air. As we watched in dismay, we saw a second plane fly into the adjacent tower. Within a short period of time the Pentagon had also been hit. Before long we witnessed both towers fall. With all flights grounded there was no way we were getting to D.C.

As we headed back home in a car Maggie had rented, I couldn't help but feel sadness for all the individuals and families affected by the terrorist attacks. That day would change the psychology of all Americans. The plot against our nation brought a new realization, that the dangers of the world could not only be felt on distant shores outside of the safety of American borders, but the threat to our security was here on our mainland. Terrorism was not guided by racial divides nor separated by class. For the first time even Middle Americans, with their white picket fences and two-point-five children seemingly safe in the heartland of America, now felt fearful and uneasy about the future.

Heading back toward Omaha where the ghetto still remained that I had momentarily emerged from, I recalled enduring threats that had always been there.

Pictures of terrorists wearing garments on their heads wielding semi-automatic weapons was a visual that was all too reminiscent of violence that residents of America's ghettos had long been accustomed to. After the threat of Al-Qaeda would long be in the background, and Americans returned to sensations of safety as they passed through airport security, the forgotten would still live in fear of the daily occurrences of misguided violence. My neighbors would still lock their doors at night for fear of their homes being invaded by thugs wearing hooded sweatshirts laced tight, while hiding desperate faces.

As the United States military forces were preparing to mobilize to fight the ideology of terror abroad, once again we had been forgotten. Soon combat boots would land on foreign shores in order to proactively prevent such atrocities as 9/11 from ever happening again, while in the meantime a similarly devastating human atrocity was taking place here at home. What a sight it would be to see grandmothers standing next to sympathetic gang members, as they waved the American flag to the sound of troops marching into the ghetto to prevent the genocide rampant within our communities. But then again maybe it was a dream too vivid for reality.

I was deeply disappointed that an opportunity that I had been looking forward to had been taken away. I had envisioned it as a great occasion to prove myself. Regardless, I remembered that everything happens for a reason, and all things have a time and a place. When one door closes, another one opens. When I returned home, I was determined to be waiting outside that door ready to sprint inside.

> "When one door closes, another one opens. When I returned home, I was determined to be waiting outside that door ready to sprint inside."

Mr. Blake had kept in contact with me and continued to take me to school regardless of where I lived. All he would talk about is how my mother was going to go to rehab, and how she missed me and that I should be with her. He started to sound like a broken record. After giving her so many chances, I had become numb toward her physical well-being. Mentally, I had prepared myself for that day when I would receive a phone call informing me that her addiction had gotten the best of her.

While I had been staying with my sister, my mother had lost her apartment again. At the rate she was going it was only a matter of time. Around the same time, my sister had started to intimately become more involved with a drug dealer she had met in high school while living in Detroit. On a clear and warm summer day he drove me around Omaha in his brand new Corvette with the top down. I thought about how one day I wouldn't mind driving my own two-seater with the top off around the city on a perfect day. I didn't personally know anyone who had achieved the lifestyle that I aspired to other than those who sold drugs.

For me the lure of selling drugs was undeniable. But even with all the seemingly glamorous aspects of a lifestyle that involves selling drugs, there were certain aspects that continued to keep me from fully choosing that path. I carefully watched my sister, who had developed a drug problem of her own. She had extreme episodes of paranoia and I had become worried about her.

She was walking down a dark path that my mother had taught us both would lead to a dead end. Regardless of what benefits the lifestyle of a successful drug dealer involved, the negatives always overpowered any benefits that I felt I would gain. All I wanted to do was to focus solely on school. The issue was that it continued to be difficult to focus on school while I had so many other more immediate issues to deal with.

Sophomore year flew by, and by staying with my sister my grades had markedly improved. Late on a school night in April, to my surprise I received a phone call from Maggie, and I had been rescheduled to speak at another MENTOR event that summer. As I pulled out my old speech and blew off the dust, I thought about how crazy fate could be. Chances missed rarely come back around for a second time. I was as hungry as I had ever been, and I knew better than to take the opportunity for granted.

A few months later my palms were sweating and I felt as if my heartbeat was the loudest thing in the large dining hall. I was a nervous inner-city high school kid who had never been to an event this nice. The actor Tom Cruise and basketball great Bill Russell were even in attendance. It was June 2002 and we were in New York City. It would be my first time speaking in front of a crowd of close to a thousand people.

This was my second attempt to deliver this speech on behalf of Congressman Osborne, with the first being on September 11, 2001, which appropriately had been postponed following the terrorist attacks. I thought about how lucky I was to even be here, and how destiny had closed one door and opened another. I had read over this speech a thousand times. It was hard to realize the magnitude of the opportunity before me, and more than anything I wanted to seize the moment.

I eyed my speech as I sat next to Emme Aronson, acknowledged as the first plus-size model. Maggie wished me luck as I got up from the table and walked to the side of the stage with Mollie in anticipation of our introduction. It wasn't long before our introduction was over, and in the midst of the applause I had mentally carved out a tunnel among the clamor for the free flow of my thoughts. Before I walked on the stage I prayed and imagined my father escorting me to the podium. I took a deep breath and read from the script that I had written:

From the start I was expected to lose. Everything I have now is mostly because I defied what the world concluded about me before I could even speak a word in my defense, and my defense is that I am just as capable as any person to do great things. Like you, I think about all the things this world could achieve if only every child were given the right tools. Mentoring is the right tool and it is the way to the American Dream.

> "My past had given me the strength that would be necessary to prepare me for my future."

When I returned from New York, public speaking opportunities started to come from every direction. I jumped at the chance to speak to kids who came from similar circumstances as mine. It was my opportunity to tell my story, to inspire, and to give hope to my generation. I wasn't looking for a handout, and I didn't want sympathy from anyone. My past had given me the strength that would be necessary to prepare me for my future. I knew my father was looking down on me, and I was dogged in my quest to actualize our dream.

7

THE RIVER STYX

Paying the ferryman my ample fare in grey hair, I climbed
into the boat and dark shores disappeared.

With me I carried nothing but the hopes of those which
despaired, and on the sands of barren lands I left behind
all fear.

The Charon dipped his oar in the river in attempt to steer,
and we slowly waded across fighting currents full of tears.

From the riverbed of the dead came cries painful to the ear, as I
asked the guide the time because I knew that mine was near.

My junior year of high school I moved back with my mother after she had supposedly been clean for a while. My sister fell on hard times and moved back in with us also. We stayed in a small two-bedroom apartment near downtown that awkwardly was located on the top of a duplex. The foundation of the entire building was faulty and unlevel. You could place a marble in one corner of the house and watch it roll clear to the other side.

The apartment was also badly infested with vermin, more so than I had ever experienced before. I was embarrassed because of where we lived and didn't want any of my friends coming over to see my living conditions. My mother also had initially failed to tell us that two drug addicts had overdosed and died in the house shortly before we moved in.

As my sister and I would soon discover, once again nothing with my mother had changed. If anything she had reached an all-time low. She had a new boyfriend named Paul who wasn't worth the two shoes on his feet. He was also a drug addict and disabled, so that physically and financially he didn't help our situation any. In fact, he made things dramatically worse.

I got into confrontations with him numerous times for wearing my clothes and shoes without my permission. I eventually found out that he would also put his hands on my mother on different occasions. Even with all that I had already endured, these would be the moments that would define my inner strength.

While my sister was staying with us, she had taken a trip with her drug dealing boyfriend, and they both had been arrested in Arizona while he was in possession of $300,000 in cash. When Tara finally came back, her drug usage and paranoia became overwhelming. I often would come home from school to find her sitting in the window filling a notebook with license plate numbers from cars she thought were involved in a plot by the FBI to send her to jail.

> "I feared that she was taking that long journey down that long murky path of lost hope."

Such a plot, however real or imaginary, never came into fruition. I was worried about her. I feared that she was taking that long journey down that long murky path of lost hope. I could tell that her last ounce of strength had long been sucked from her spirit.

As always, it wasn't long before my sister and my mother started to argue. My sister moved back out as soon as she got the chance. As a result I was usually at the house by myself. My mother had stopped grocery shopping altogether, and I depended on school lunch to get me through the day. It was hard to think about my college dreams or any test that was in front of me when hunger consumed me. If I wasn't already a man, this would be the moment of my maturation.

Dealing with my mother had become increasingly more difficult. My mother's addiction had elevated to a new plateau. She had become so hopelessly entrapped in her obsession with crack that I had no idea who she was anymore. She had made a habit of running off and leaving me at home alone for weeks at a time. After making phone calls to discover her whereabouts, my search would usually lead me to my Aunt Trish's high-rise apartment.

Aunt Trish's apartment was roughly a half-hour walk from where we lived. The apartment was a haven for the poor and physically or mentally disabled. When physical or mental ailments accompany poverty, drugs are often never far behind, and the building was a gold mine for those who sold drugs.

After making the walk to my aunt's apartment, I would usually brush past a group of distraught figures who stood hunched over in front of the building doorway, and likely would never escape the gravity of that cold concrete that unwillingly had been molded to their feet. I dialed my aunt's number from a black phone next to the entry way so she could come down and let me inside.

As I waited and looked through the glass door into the building lobby, a bell would unexpectedly chime as someone would exit the elevator, and other solemn faces would suddenly stir and look up in my direction, as if momentarily awakened from a bad dream. After staring through the glass at me for a few seconds, they would put their heads back down possibly realizing simultaneously that I was neither their savior nor had their bad dream come to an end. Possessing physical and mental disabilities, they shared the plight of the forgotten.

When my aunt finally walked off the elevator, she opened the door, releasing a sudden burst of air filled with odors that triggered familiar memories. They were smells that reminded me of the stuffy hospital hallways I often visited whenever my mother received medical treatment for her sickle-cell. When I stepped inside the lobby and got a closer look at my aunt, I could see that her drug usage had reduced her to a state beyond my recognition.

But regardless of what she wore or how untidy her hair may have been, I always hugged her fully and gave her the utmost respect. She was a weathered rock that had seen many things in her lifetime, and if nothing else the wisdom she often shared was worth more to me than riches. She couldn't tell me which way to go, but from her own extensive experience she often advised me regarding which paths led to a dead end.

Before she had moved in with us during my youth, she had sold cocaine in Minneapolis. Making over a thousand dollars a day in profits, the person I saw before me had once been entirely different. After a while, like many of those who sell drugs she began to use them as well. Her drug usage had partly led her to be the image that I now saw standing in front of me.

As we stepped onto the elevator, I began to hold my breath while attempting to avoid the faint smell of urine that filled my nostrils. Finally, we arrived at our destination on the eighth floor. When we got off the elevator, Aunt Trish told me to wait while she fetched my mother. As I waited in the narrow and stifling hallway for her to return, I looked out of the window down at the parking lot eight stories below.

I felt that life had yet to be kind and I wondered if I would be missed. I longed to be in the presence of my father again, but I knew it couldn't be now. I wasn't going to quit. There were too many people relying on me.

While I had been pondering to myself, I heard a voice behind me. It was my mother. Looking at her I broke down inside as her stained clothes barely hung onto her scanty frame, and her collar bone protruded from her skin as if she had barely eaten in weeks. The expression on her face reminded me of a child who knew that she had done something wrong.

> "I'd call out for someone, anyone, only to hear the reply of nothingness."

After eventually getting her back home, every once in a while I would crack her bedroom door open to make sure that she was still there. A few days would pass and I would come home from school, and after closing the front door I'd call out for someone, anyone, only to hear the reply of nothingness. And just like that, she would be gone again.

As a youth who could be described as the stereotypical socioeconomically disadvantaged young Black male in America, I would be forced to sink or swim. There were no special accommodations for those disproportionately burdened by the trials of poverty. There were no grading systems involving curves to offset the hardships of growing up in the single-parent household of a drug addict. I received no special academic attention because my primary school education had been unequal to that of many of my more privileged peers.

I thought it to be unfair that I was expected to excel at the same pace as my more fortunate classmates, while still being forced to deal with so many other issues outside of the classroom. But no one owed me anything. I had no choice but to hop on one leg and juggle bowling pins, while simultaneously performing at the same academic level as everyone else. I was given no other option.

This was the hand I had been dealt, and it was the same hand that my father similarly had been forced to play in his youth. The sensation of relief brought by stability was the Heaven I was seeking, but I'd have to cross the River Styx first to get there. I had made up my mind that I wouldn't become a victim of my circumstances.

Around this time I came to depend almost solely on myself. I woke myself up for school every day, while suppressing thoughts that I didn't have to go. In the end who would reprimand me? I quickly learned how to cook for myself. I was faced with either learning how to be self-sufficient or simply going hungry.

At times it came to the point that there was nothing to eat besides canned goods. One evening in particular, I opened up the cupboard and all that was left was a single can of Spam. I couldn't stand Spam but there were no alternatives. As I opened the can and reached for the timer on the microwave, I jumped back in disgust.

Roaches had congregated on the inside of the microwave so densely that they covered up the digital numbers of the timer. Some believe that in this life you pay for all of the mistakes that you've made in your former life. If this was the case, then I had doubly paid for any mistakes I had previously made, and then some.

My mother had also stopped paying the bills, and our landlord would knock on our door at least twice a week. Usually all that I could tell him was the truth, which was that I didn't have the slightest idea regarding her whereabouts. One night as I sat home alone in the living room doing my homework, the electricity was cut off. My strength was waning and mentally I had moved beyond fatigue.

Who knew where my mother was or when the last time was that she had paid the electric bill? I tried to search the house looking for candles, but I couldn't find any. I contemplated sitting right there in the middle of my living room floor and giving up. No matter how well I did or how hard I tried, I just couldn't catch a break. All I could do was fall down to my knees in the pitch black and pray.

I realized that I didn't possess any traditional talents so I knew that school was my only way out. I was determined to finish my homework that night, and I wasn't going to let my situation stop me. Combing the house, I ran across rubbing alcohol in the bathroom cabinet. I went into the kitchen and poured the rubbing alcohol into a martini glass. After finding a lighter, I lit the alcohol for reading light.

I opened up my books and as my vision became blurry from the tears, I promised myself that, no matter what, not only was I going to escape my situation, but my children would never have to endure the things I had. I thought about my father and how much different things would have been had he been alive during that moment. He first dreamed of escaping poverty, reaching stability, and using stability as a launch pad to change the course of his destiny. Now it was up to me to keep my father's dream alive, and I was determined to keep it alive through any means necessary.

The neighborhood that we lived in was as much downtown as it was in South Omaha. The south part of town was largely Hispanic and was just as bad as many parts of North Omaha. In some aspects it was worse. It was the Spanish ghetto.

As I walked to the corner store, I could see people brawling with baseball bats. I was often approached by prostitutes while walking to school in the early morning hours. However unconventional it may have been, this was my life. A life that was all that I knew and had ever known. I became obsessed with trying to find a way to leave it all behind.

This year Christmas would prove to be bittersweet. My mother finally decided to show up and took me to the Salvation Army where they were handing out gifts to the less fortunate. We waited in line along with countless other families who were latching onto hopes that Christmas wouldn't pass them by this year.

Finally, we arrived at the section inside a gymnasium designated for picking out gifts, and it seemed as if we had arrived too late. Most of the gifts were already gone, and only those that were least desirable were left behind. It wasn't a secret that I didn't want to be there. It was a humiliating and humbling reminder that I was poor. I grabbed a disappointing gift and we left.

My mother had also signed us up to receive gifts from a family who would adopt us for Christmas. On Christmas day as I unwrapped my present from the Salvation Army and pretended to be surprised, there was a knock on the door. My mother instructed me to answer it.

When I opened up the door, a middle-aged white gentleman was standing outside with a small girl who appeared to be his daughter. I invited them inside and they placed a few gifts under our modest tree. We thanked them, and my mother engaged in conversation with the gentleman until they left shortly thereafter.

I was appreciative and thankful that I had received anything at all, but the feeling of constantly being on the receiving end of charity is one that I would wish on no man. Regardless, I quickly remembered other years when I had received nothing at all and I was thankful. The experience put me in the habit of never expecting anything from anyone. That way it was impossible to ever be disappointed. If I was going to make it, I would have to depend on myself, and I was determined to make it on my own two feet.

Toward the end of my junior year of high school, prom was around the corner. With everything that was going on at home I looked forward to a moment of refuge, however brief. Our school allowed juniors as well as seniors to attend and all my friends were going.

At the time I had been dating a girl who lived in my old neighborhood in the Miller Park area. It was undeniable that she was one of the most beautiful girls I had dated up until that point. Like me she had come from a broken home, and as the oldest child of many she was often confined to her home, attempting to take on the role of a matriarch to the best of her ability.

When she wasn't taking care of her younger brothers or sisters, she found refuge in the streets. She never discussed her dreams or ambitions, more than likely an effort to shield herself from disappointment like so many other young people who endured similar circumstances. She had never been outside the city limits of Omaha. She reminded me of youth in large metropolitan areas who due to the smog, tall buildings, and light pollution had never seen the stars. In either case it is extremely difficult to reach for something you don't know is there.

I had issues with the way she scantily dressed. She admired the video vixens like so many other young Black women her age. To them their bodies were more likely to give them the tools to escape poverty before their self-worth ever would. Having a light complexion, the world along with the media told her that her Anglo-Saxon features made her more attractive than her brown-skinned ethnic-looking counterparts. She naively believed it.

She was a rebel, constantly getting kicked out of class in the low performing high school she attended on the other side of town. She consistently fought because the world told her she was beautiful, and in order for her to be beautiful, her peers who exhibited more African features had to be ugly, and consequently the false ideology bred jealously. Someone had done their job well. I knew the ghetto wasn't strong enough to contain me, and I thought I could inspire her to also take flight.

Prom night wasn't very eventful. I didn't drink, smoke, and was not yet intent on losing my virginity. I had borrowed my cousin Bianca's car to get around that night. After the dance was over and we joined a few of my friends to grab a bite to eat at a favorite after-hours restaurant, I drove her home.

Pulling up in front of her house in the early morning hours, deep in the heart of the ghetto, I kissed her goodnight. As she stepped out of the car and shut the door, our futures would instantly head in polarized directions.

Two days after prom I would find out that she was in the hospital and had survived two gunshot wounds below the waist. She had been another victim who had been in the wrong place at the wrong time. But then again, bullets never had any names on them.

Still possessing negative attitudes toward her own self-worth, as soon as she would turn eighteen she would head toward Los Angeles to pursue a career in adult entertainment. It was a career that would be short lived as she returned home to raise her child as a single mother. One child quickly multiplied and before my own eyes I would witness the cycle of poverty that I sought so desperately to discontinue once again prevail.

Her story wasn't any different from that of numerous other young Black women throughout America who lack father figures to provide them with an example of unconditional love from a man and who also lack self-esteem as they vainly pursue a concept of beauty that is physically impossible to ever achieve. It was a blatant reminder that I wasn't alone in my struggle.

The summer before my senior year, I ran across an information packet about a summer program focusing on international relations and domestic politics. The program would be held at some of the most prestigious universities around the country. The program was called the Junior Statesmen Program of America. For some time, I had already started to develop a deep love for politics. I saw politics as an avenue for becoming a catalyst for change. It had become my dream to help the downtrodden, regardless of race, because I knew poverty has no color. Maybe this program could feed my political inclinations.

The program cost over four thousand dollars, and I had no idea how I would pay for it. No one in my family had any money to give. I thought it unfair how I could be held back from my ambitions by my financial situation.

As I discussed my grievances with my mentor Maggie, she reminded me that my mentoring program had money set aside for each participant that would be accessible upon our high school graduation. She suggested that I contact MENTOR who was in control of the money and ask for the necessary funds to be prematurely distributed to me so that I could attend the summer program. After anxiously waiting for a few weeks my request had been approved, and once again mentoring had come through.

Early during the summer before my senior year I arrived at Reagan National Airport. I had chosen to attend the Junior Statesmen Summer Program at Georgetown University in Washington, D.C. James was there waiting at the terminal to pick me up. He was tall and bald with a brown complexion and a preppy look. He was the vice president of MENTOR and had been responsible for giving me my first opportunity to speak in New York. He had served as my mentor and role model ever since.

The three-week program was a hot spot for the children of America's upper crest. The overwhelming majority were headed straight for Harvard, Princeton, and Yale. I immediately stood out like a sore thumb. The program was extremely rigorous comprising of college-level courses in government, international relations, and debate. It also included a meticulous writing portion, and I quickly found my educational background to be inadequate in order to compete on the same level as everyone else. Yet, I was highly competitive and refused to be left behind. I had been lucky enough to have Maggie loan me her laptop computer, and without it I would have been seriously handicapped.

On a Saturday, James picked me up in his green Jeep Wrangler and gave me a tour of Howard University. It was the shining glory of academia in Black America. I had never met anyone who had ever gone to Howard, so I didn't even think it was ever an option for me. Where I had come from I'd get a standing ovation if I graduated from high school and attended any college at all. I didn't think I had any chance of getting in and put any thought of attending the institution into the back of my mind for the time being.

Toward the end of the program, I started to excel in debate, writing, and analytical thinking. The fact that I was outperforming those who were fortunate enough to have been given everything necessary in order to secure their success gave me a huge boost in confidence. Now I knew that I had the ability to perform with some of America's best, and it was time for me to think about where I would be headed a year from now. Since I performed well in the program, maybe I had what it took to get into Howard University. In my mind Howard was still a long shot, and before I thought about the future I would have to return home and deal with the barriers of my present.

8

SHOOTING FOR THE STARS

Looking up at the stars, I imagined that in me was the
agility to defy Newton's law of gravity.

Traveling through the abyss of space faster than the speed of
sunshine, I shattered theories posed by Albert Einstein;

I sped past Mars, toward where clouds of nebulae engulf
quasars and white dwarf stars.

Escaping a world that I swore would never again find me, my
emancipation from deprivation would come to define me.

౿ౡ

My senior year rolled around, and my sister had gotten back on her feet again. I was beyond enthused to move back in with her and leave behind the prior situation that I had been living in. My sister's new place was a two-bedroom apartment that was located in another small low-income housing complex. We were still in the ghetto but it couldn't be as bad as living with my mother.

Tara spent the first week bombing the apartment in an attempt to kill all the vermin. Eventually she would succeed, and the apartment would turn out to be a pretty decent place notwithstanding its location. Mr. Blake still kept in close contact with me and still took me to school every day. I was finally able to fully focus on school again, and my thirst to take flight from the ghetto overwhelmed my consciousness.

Upward Bound was a program aimed at getting first-generation and low-income students into college, regardless of their race. I had first become involved with the program in the eighth grade and had been determined to stick with it. The program provided after-school tutoring, college tours, and an academic summer aspect where college-level courses were offered. It was a highly efficient program in that it kept all of us out of trouble and surrounded us with students from similar backgrounds who had the ambition and the drive to want more.

During my senior year the program had become critically pivotal in my quest to escape. The program paid for all of our standardized testing, college applications, and even the postage to mail them. Everything I had been through had taken a toll on my grades, and by the time I was a senior my grade point average was a subpar 2.9 accumulative. My standardized test scores proved to be above average. Neither my grades nor test scores were phenomenal enough to get any academic scholarships.

My family of course didn't have any money, so I needed to figure out a way to pay for college. After filling out the FAFSA forms for financial aid, our estimated family contribution was zero. Regardless, I was still determined to go to college. The only other way for me to get there would be to fill out as many scholarship applications as I could get my hands on. If that's what it was going to take.

Every day after school, I faithfully walked over to the offices of the Upward Bound program at Creighton University—the same school my father had attended for law school. They gave me access to their typewriter, printers, and computers, which were everything that I would need. I usually stayed until the last person would leave the office.

I frequently made trips to my high school counselor's office during my lunch period to look for new scholarships. I constantly searched the Internet for every applicable scholarship I could find. There was no plan B for me. Eventually, I would go on to apply for sixty-seven different scholarships before the school year ended.

When I wasn't busy writing essays for scholarship applications, I was filling out applications for admission to various universities. None of the schools that I applied to were in Nebraska. I knew that if I stayed in Nebraska, especially with my family situation, there would be no way that I would be able to stay focused.

Because I refused to stay in Nebraska, this also took a large toll on the number of scholarships that I could apply for, due to the fact that many of them required me to stay in state. There were too many distractions at home, and I knew that I needed to leave. I didn't want to leave my family behind, but if I would ever be able to save them, I would have to save myself first.

Of all the colleges that I had applied to, I was intent on attending Howard University. My heart had been set on attending Howard since I had visited the campus during the previous summer while attending the Junior Statesmen Program at Georgetown. On a weekday I went to my mother's house to pick up my mail when I discovered that I had a letter from Howard.

My mother wasn't home as usual. She had predictably failed to be involved in my college application process, which wasn't abnormal as she was usually busy dealing with her own issues. I only knew that she wanted me to stay close to home and go to school.

Before I opened the letter, I kneeled down on both knees and prayed. I just hoped someone would be listening. Repetitiously tapping my fingers on the envelope, I was scared to open it. I finally ripped opened the letter and learned I had been accepted! I had been looking for a way out and this was it. Now that I knew where I was going, I had to figure out how I was going to pay for it.

The results from my scholarship applications started to roll in. I received nine scholarships in all. None of them were full academic scholarships but I had received enough aid to get me through the first year at least. I also still had a few thousand dollars from my mentoring program. It seemed like things were finally starting to come together.

One scholarship in particular required an essay portion discussing what I would do if I were President. Over eight thousand students submitted entries and only fifty of them were accepted. I made the local newspaper a second time for being one of the winners. In the article I discussed my possible political ambitions and talked somewhat in depth about my background and life at home. Some of my relatives were upset about the article, but I didn't pay the criticisms any attention because I didn't do anything other than tell the truth.

I knew for a fact that many of my cousins were enduring the same things that I was going through. It takes one person to be unselfish to sacrifice everything in order to provide a foundation for future generations to build off. That one person had been my father, and when he died, the foundation that he had built crumbled. It was up to me to rebuild that foundation, in order to make the journey toward upward mobility easier for my children and others around me.

Graduation came before I knew it, and a few of my close family members were there to support me. It felt good when I walked across the stage to receive my diploma, but it didn't fill my void of assurance. I knew that although graduating from high school was an accomplishment, I still had a long way to go.

My Aunt Mary Ann was in town from Kansas City and took me out to eat. But overall, a big deal wasn't made about my graduation. My mother didn't do anything special for me, but that was expected. I knew where all her money and time were being spent. Since I couldn't rely on my mother for the necessary encouragement, I had to create my own if I was going to stay motivated.

That night after everyone had parted ways, I drove alone to Council Bluffs to the cemetery where my father was buried. I kept the car running with the lights on, and after rolling the window down I stepped outside into the night. Accompanied by a cool breeze, the darkness was ubiquitous. My Aunt Mary Ann had taken me there once before when I was younger, and I had still remembered the way.

As I struggled to find his plot again, I had the feeling that I was in the cemetery alone. After rediscovering it, I fell to my knees and brushed the dust and fallen leaves off the headstone of my father who had come before me. I had come to pay homage to the fallen. I brought all of the awards that I had won, a graduation announcement, and my cap as my sacrifice to the dead.

I laid them neatly in front of his headstone. I couldn't help but miss him, and I regretted that he couldn't be there to see how far I had come or where I was headed. I promised to take care of my mom and sister while he was gone. And more than anything I promised to continue to breathe life into our dream.

The summer before college, I purposefully tried to make those two and a half months as uneventful as possible. I didn't want to get into any trouble that would mess things up for me. During the first part of the summer I was fortunate enough to have Upward Bound pay for me to take a college algebra course at a local university in Omaha. During the second half of the summer I landed an internship working at the state office of Nebraska's United States Senator Ben Nelson, and coming straight out of high school I would become their youngest intern ever.

I used my Aunt Mary Ann's car to get to and from school and work. The car she had given me had been in a pretty serious wreck. Although the body wasn't damaged too badly, the passenger and driver's side airbags had deployed, and she never had it fixed. I didn't care how the car looked. I was just happy that I had a way to get to work and school.

While interning in Ben Nelson's state office, I was heavily influenced by a personable woman named Felicia Dillon and a very honorable man by the name of Sonny Foster. Sonny Foster had even been well acquainted with my father. They both took me under their wing and helped foster my love for politics. My experience there fueled my excitement to be in Washington, D.C., even more.

That summer I had discovered that my mother had tried to forge and cash my payroll checks, which were still being mailed to her address. I was so surprised that I didn't even know how to feel about it. I knew the drugs had taken over who she really was, but I was hurt that my own mother would steal from me.

It was at moments like this that I thought of my father. Since he wasn't there, I felt like the only way that I could make things better was by taking on his role. I had to strengthen my family by taking on the role of a patriarch. I had to find a way to progress and help everyone do better.

The entire summer I still was living with my sister. On a summer day during the weekend I sat in my bedroom talking on the phone, when my sister knocked on my door and walked in. I got off the phone as she sat down on the edge of my bed, and there was an awkward silence. After a few moments she told me that she was pregnant.

She had been dating a new guy, whom I had met once or twice. I never approved of her taste in men. In my mind I thought what else could go wrong? She was twenty-five at the time, so her age wasn't the issue. She wasn't married, and the guy she was dating was a deadbeat who already had enough kids of his own.

At that point I asked her what she planned to do. She hesitated for a second and then responded that she was going to keep it. From that point on I knew that I would be on my own and that things would never be the same. Once the baby was born, she wouldn't be able to help support me like she used to.

I was happy that I was going to have a nephew or niece, but it definitely worried me how I would get by without her help. Maybe it was time for me to grow up and learn to be independent. After all she had given up a lot to help me get as far as I had gotten.

My sister was also dating a Polish man whom she often used for money. She was living a fast life, while subconsciously following my mother's footsteps down a path of ruin. It seemed that my sister had inherited the very aspects of our mother that she promised herself she'd never be.

> "I wondered what it would be like to not be me, and what the ultimate price for normalcy would be."

Her want for more would eventually catch up with her. The same Polish man my sister had been dating had bought her a fairly new luxury car. My sister regularly bragged to friends and our family about it. Then one day he unexpectedly came to the house and took the car back.

My sister tried to fight him over the car. When the police arrived, she tried to fight them too. All the while as her arms flung wild, her thoughts had failed to take into account her unborn child. I wondered what it would be like to not be me, and what the ultimate price for normalcy would be.

The end of the summer came, and it was finally time for me to go to Howard. My mother could barely take care of herself, so I didn't expect her to play any significant part in helping to get me there. I had been lucky that my Aunt Mary Ann and a few of my cousins just so happened to be heading to D.C. for unrelated reasons. I packed up everything that I could fit into the car my Aunt Mary Ann had loaned me. I made a few farewell visits prior to departing Omaha and before I was scheduled meet everyone at my aunt's home in Kansas City, Missouri.

The last stop that I made before heading down to Kansas City would be my Aunt Trish's apartment. It was conveniently located next to the Interstate heading toward Missouri. I pulled up in front of the building where I had so often come to drag my mother from and vainly fought back dark memories that brutally suffocated all other thoughts that were swirling around in my mind. My Aunt Trish was already waiting outside for me.

She greeted me with the same welcoming smile that had brought me comfort since she had first walked through our front door during the early days of my childhood. As usual, the clothes she wore were worn beyond their time. Her hair contained sporadic streaks of gray from the stress of an everlasting struggle, and her figure had been warped by the drugs and lifestyle that she hopelessly latched onto. The miserable combination made her appear aged far beyond her natural years.

I wrapped my arms around her and at the same time embraced one who had forever had my back, like a rear gunner in mid-flight during fierce dogfights at night when the clouds blotted out all starlight. I clutched onto her tighter and my emotions finally burst through the dam of a hardened heart, as we both wept while standing in the empty parking lot. After I regained my composure, she placed her hand upon my brow and began to pray.

> "On the long journey ahead toward the realization of my dreams, there would be little time for tears."

Her prayer filled me with a burning determination and a confidence renewed. On the long journey ahead toward the realization of my dreams, there would be little time for tears. As I drove off and wished her goodbye, I was more ambitious than ever.

As I reached the outside of the city limits and began to pass through the country side, in my rear view I could still see the city's meager skyline. I had made it out of the ghetto, but as long as my family and others I had known were still struggling, such thoughts failed to bring me relief. Heading down the highway I imagined that my craft mocked the laws of physics, as I passed through the stratosphere shooting for stars flickering near the edge of the universe beyond. The road I now embarked on involved a mission greater than myself, and I prayed for the strength to carry on.

Aunt Mary Ann lived in one of the worst neighborhoods in Kansas City, Missouri. Her house was white with chipped paint barely hanging onto aged wood siding, likely dating from the turn of the twentieth century. On either side of her house sat abandoned boarded-up homes, a sign of the decomposing conditions in a neighborhood that so many sought to escape. Although I had traveled hundreds of miles to flee from my own misery, it was a reminder of how the plight of the forgotten was omnipresent.

She often called police on misguided youth who sold crack in front of her house. As a result of her rebellion and efforts to protect the sanctity of her neighborhood, she had become a target of those whose flow of income she was interrupting. Her house had been broken into and vandalized more times than I can remember. During the most recent act of burglary, her dog had been shot and killed inside the confines of her home. I hated to see her live in that unforgiving environment, but I knew that the first step in any plot to help her escape would be for me to finish school.

By the time I arrived, my older cousins had already rented a minivan, and we were all ready to begin the

long trip ahead. When we were finally on the road
headed toward Washington, D.C., we had managed to
pack all of my belongings into the van, along with my
aunt, four of my cousins, and a German Shepherd. If
you could imagine it was an extremely uncomfortable
twenty-one-hour drive. I tried to sleep most of the way
so that time would go by more quickly.

The last leg of the trip I drove, and before I knew
it we were in the nation's capital. I had never driven
in such a large city before, and the high amount of
traffic made me nervous. After about fifteen minutes
of navigating through the district, we pulled up to the
curb in front of the dormitory where I would be staying
for the next nine months, Drew Hall. The dormitory
was an all-male dorm named after Charles R. Drew,
an African American physician and surgeon, whose
ground-breaking research involving new methods of
storing large quantities blood had saved countless lives
during World War II.

I put the car in park and stepped into the warm sun to
get my things. I took a moment to look around and take
it all in. I was unused to seeing so many Black people in
one place at one time. It was an empowering sight to see
countless youth focused on higher education bustling
to and fro that resembled me. I noticed students called
"Campus Pals" wearing navy blue shirts, with odd names
on the back, helping the newly arrived students carry
their belongings in large orange bins.

A few of the Campus Pals, along with my cousins,

helped me carry my belongings to my room. I quickly checked in, and sooner than I had expected, my aunt and cousins were kissing and hugging me goodbye. Before I knew it, I was alone sitting on a bare twin bed staring out the window.

> "In an effort to chase my dreams I had left my small shallow pond and leaped into an ocean, and I would have no choice but to find a way to stay afloat."

Although I was happy to be there, I was fearful at the same time. I was in an entirely new environment now, alone. My sister wouldn't be a phone call away to save me if I needed her. But I knew that my mentor James would be in the city, which brought me a little comfort. In an effort to chase my dreams I had left my small shallow pond and leaped into an ocean, and I would have no choice but to find a way to stay afloat.

The first semester I made friends quickly, but there were few whom I truly identified with. Most of my classmates were middle-class Blacks, many whose parents and grandparents had also attended Howard. Most people naturally gravitated toward others who were geographically from similar regions of the country. But because I was the only person that I knew from Nebraska, it was tough to find my place at first.

More than anything I spent the bulk of my time in the library. James had been kind enough to purchase a laptop for me when I arrived. Without his assistance I have no idea how I would have been able to make it through school. I walked to class with tunnel vision intent on what I had come to do. I had come so far and I was determined to do whatever it took to keep making progress.

It was a hope of mine that I would be able to get a scholarship for my education next year in order to pay for my tuition since none of my previous scholarships I had received during my senior year of high school had been renewable. My first semester went by quickly and my grades came back promising. I had scored A's and B's in all of my classes and had even made the Dean's list. I had finally gotten the opportunity that I had always wanted, and I was doing my best to seize it.

When I went home that Christmas, my sister had given birth to a baby girl a few weeks before I had arrived. I was happy that she had decided not to get an abortion. My niece was the single most beautiful thing I had ever seen. It felt good to be back in a familiar setting, while surrounded by familiar faces. My first semester had been tough socially, but even with that being said I was ready to return to school. It wasn't hard to tell that there wasn't anything at home for me. My mother hadn't changed her ways, and my sister planned on moving back to Detroit within the next month.

During my time home I looked forward to spending time with my friends who were also home from college. We all sought to enjoy our break after a semester of hard work. Soon New Year's had sneaked up on us, and it would be one that neither I nor any of my friends would ever forget. I had thought once I went to college that trouble wouldn't be able to find me. I was far from right.

Late at night during the first hour of the New Year, all of my closest high school friends were riding in the car with me: Shannon, Austin, and Aendre. My Aunt Mary Ann had given me her extra car again to drive while back home. It was the same totaled car that I had after my high school graduation to get back and forth from school and my congressional internship with Senator Ben Nelson the previous summer.

That night I was the designated driver, being that I was the only one out of my group of friends who still had never consumed alcohol before. I had become accustomed to playing the role of the designated driver after our late-night outings. After we finally brought in the New Year at a friend's house, we all were ready to head to the next location. We heard about a party at another friend's house on the other side of town and decided to stop by.

As I walked outside with my car keys in my hand, I saw a woman backing up a small sport utility vehicle up a steep incline in the direction of my car. Before I could get her attention, she backed right into my driver's side front bumper. I ran up the street to the scene of the accident and discovered my car had no damage.

Her vehicle had a huge dent at the point of impact. She didn't want to exchange insurance in an attempt to keep her insurance premium down. I didn't mind because I didn't see any damage to my aunt's car, and technically the car was already totaled.

Trying not to let the small mishap ruin our night, in no time my friends and I were back in my car headed toward our friend's house, which just so happened to be in one of the nicest neighborhoods in the city. On the way there my friend Austin had gone far beyond his drinking limit. He had his head leaning out the open window on the passenger's side as we went over a speed bump.

Austin immediately vomited on the side of my aunt's car. Upset, I pulled the car over to the side of the road. Austin got out and tried to clean the car off while I told him to get back inside. I did my best to clean up the mess and was determined not to let the incident spoil the New Year.

When we finally arrived at our friend's house, we noticed that all the lights were out. He lived on a dead end street with a circular turn-about located at the end of the street, which was also on a steep incline. We turned around at the end of the street, and I parked facing the bottom of the hill and opposite of the dead end.

It looked as if we had been given the wrong information. We called our friend and no one answered. Other friends of ours had also followed us from the last house, and everyone except Austin and me had gotten out of the car to discuss what was to be done next.

While attempting to place a bottle of wine inside a full cup of liquor, Austin spilled alcohol all over the front interior of the car. I should have never let them have open containers in the car. Irate beyond belief, I had enough and got out of the car and proceeded to walk around the passenger side of the car to pull Austin out. All of a sudden I noticed that the car was rolling down the hill!

In a rush to get Austin out of the car, I had been absent-minded and had forgotten to put the car in park. Austin was still inside the car when I ran back to the front driver's side door. I attempted to put my foot on the brake to stop the car, but it was already moving too fast. Simultaneously, Austin jumped out of the passenger's side of the car and rolled on the ground like a scene from a James Bond movie.

> "I saw all my dreams rolling down the hill into the night along with the car."

Helplessly, all I could do was watch in horror as the car ran over a mailbox and continued careening down the street. I couldn't believe what was happening. The car ran over a small tree in a neighbor's yard and then continued rolling down the block headed across the intersecting street. My entire life flashed before my eyes, and all I could think about was how everything I had ever worked for was over. I saw all my dreams rolling down the hill into the night along with the car, as it ran through a row of bushes and hit the front of a house across the street.

In an odd twist of fate the car had hit the only small portion of the house that had been built with bricks. As I sat dumbfounded for a few seconds that the car didn't go through the house, and before I could even think about what I was doing, my legs were carrying me toward the car like my life depended on it. I jumped in the driver's seat and put the key in the ignition to start the car, and that night the stars and planets must have been aligned because the engine ignited.

I pulled away from the house and out of the yard in reverse with all urgency. I put the car in drive and sped away with my heart pounding at a thousand beats per second. Following my lead, I saw my friends in the rear view mirror get in their cars as quickly as they could. I drove around for fifteen minutes with my mind racing and eventually pulled into a junior high parking lot to assess the car's body damage. I wiped the debris off the front of the car and realized that there was barely a scratch. I couldn't believe that I had been so careless.

Less than a week later I had driven the car back to my aunt in Kansas City and was on a plane headed back to Howard. As I sat in my seat on the airplane preparing for takeoff, I was still trying to wrap my head around what happened. I deeply regretted the damage we had done. I vowed never to put my future or my dreams in jeopardy again.

Second semester of my freshman year was the exact opposite of the first. I became more involved in various organizations and quite honestly I became too involved.

My grades dropped dramatically and I spent a lot less time in the library. I felt more comfortable being away from home and made a lot more friends. But as a result, I started to forget what I had come there for.

I didn't have any excuses not to be focusing on school anymore. Only months ago I had been in the ghetto. All the previous factors that had been barriers to my success were no longer there. I had started to become lax, which was the last thing that I could to do if I was going to make it. Although I had made it to college, now it was up to me to stay there.

I had come to realize that the adversity that I had experienced during the earlier part of my life had been adding fuel to my fire. Mingling with so many students who came from backgrounds that were nothing like mine, I felt as if I was starting to lose my own identity. The end of my freshman year at Howard had finally come, and I half dreaded going back home. Yet, at the same time I thought it might benefit me to be reminded of where I had come from, where I was trying to go, and the dream that I was fighting to keep alive.

When I flew home, my mother was still staying with Mr. Blake. He also had one of his children staying with us, so his small apartment was still extremely cramped. His son stayed in one bedroom while he slept on the coach and I shared a bed with my mother like I had when I was younger. I felt like I had taken ten steps backward staying at Mr. Blake's again, but at the same time I knew that it was a temporary sacrifice for a long-term gain.

I had also failed to secure a summer job before I came back home. During the day I would lie in the bed staring at the wall trying to figure out what I was going to do. Whatever it was, I had to get away from Mr. Blake's apartment. When the walls started to close in, I decided to look for a job the next day.

Just when I thought I was starting to go crazy, I received a call from my old program, Upward Bound. One of the employees for the summer program had been fired and there was an opening. I packed up my bags and was thankful.

The position that I had been given would be as a residential adviser for high school students. I lived in apartment-style dormitories along with the students. The students were all mature and old enough so that my job only required me to serve as more of a mentor. I had been in their position only a year ago, which made it easy to relate, and I tried my best to provide them with assistance in any way I could.

At the same time that I was working, I was enrolled in an accelerated Spanish and applied calculus course. I knew that foreign language and math were my weakest subjects. If I could just manage to take them during the summer at another school, as long as I received at least a C in the courses, it wouldn't affect my grade point average at Howard. I attended the Spanish course from 8 a.m. to 4 p.m. and went straight to my applied calculus course from 5 p.m. to 9 p.m. After class I went back to work at Upward Bound and stayed up late into the night doing homework.

The summer sped by and I had saved a fair amount of money. I had passed both of my classes, but the financial assistance that I had received, along with money I had saved from work, wouldn't be enough to cover my full tuition for the next school year. I had applied for and was awarded the Sallie Mae American Dream Scholarship, which I had also received during my freshman year. Even with the American Dream Scholarship I still needed more money and had no idea how I was going to get the money to go back to Howard.

Luckily Maggie's husband knew of a contractor who installed insulation and could use an extra hand. With only a few weeks left before I had to go back to school, I showed up to work faithfully every day. I started off driving an eleven-ton truck hauling workloads to project sites. Daily work consisted of climbing tall ladders and stapling insulation during the early stages of home construction. Often working in one hundred degree weather, the temperature inside of the houses was always hotter.

The last house we worked on was in one of the nicer parts of town. It was the type of house that I would always stop and admire. The house was being built from the ground up with a price tag of $1.5 million. I had never been in a house that nice, and even if I was only installing insulation, it was pure motivation to see what one person could obtain.

My only work partner was a middle-aged white man whose name escapes me. Although he had little education, he had a treasure trove of knowledge to give. Working alongside him gave me an even greater appreciation for hard-working blue-collar workers. He reminded me that the type of work we did, involving constant exposure to the dangers of asbestos, was nothing to get used to. He told me that whatever I did to make sure that I finished school. I gave him my word that I would.

Standing at the entrance of a large hall filled to capacity, I was back in New York again, not too far from where I had embarked on my first public speaking experience three years ago. It was the night of June 14, 2005, and MENTOR was holding its National Recognition Event at a gorgeous venue on the pier. I noticed Russell Simmons and Kimora Lee Simmons who had come to support Russell's brother "Rev Run," who was being acknowledged that night for his work in mentoring.

As one of the guest speakers for the night, I patiently awaited my introduction while repetitiously rehearsing my speech, going over every pause and voice inflection. This time I had painstakingly memorized every word. I saw it as another opportunity to hone my public speaking skills and speak on behalf of those who weren't present to articulate for themselves. It was another chance to bring light to the plight of the forgotten. Imaging my father standing next to me brought me comfort once again.

I adjusted my tie and straightening my suit while waiting for my introduction to end. As I was beckoned to the stage, I navigated through the dense crowd and moved toward the bright lights. Walking onto the stage resolute on grabbing ahold of the occasion before me, I shook the hand of Geoffrey Boisi, the former CEO of JPMorgan Investment Bank and, ignored the streaming words on the teleprompter, then began:

Tonight, I would like to thank individuals such as yourselves, whose ... dedication towards a cause that is greater than us all, has saved millions of lives ... Yet, I believe that we are capable of more, and that belief has developed into a vision. In this vision I have foreseen a better America ... An America where every promising child who wishes to succeed has a mentor waiting with a blueprint for success ... An America that regardless of my socio-economic background I can be anything that I aspire to be. I ask you to take this vision back to your communities and organizations with a ... newfound urgency to make this vision into something real. It is imperative that we make a difference today, because sadly there are millions of children who cannot wait for tomorrow.

Walking off the stage I was doing my part to turn a new page. I was using the world of mentoring as a catalyst for change. I represented a new generation of those who were steadfast in altering the direction of a nation. Young, ambitious, and optimistic I still had hope while many saw hope as unrealistic. I found it hard to become accepting of the status quo, and every single time that I addressed the world, I was going to let the world know.

The summer had sped by, and before I knew it there was one week left before I would return to school. Although my job installing insulation had helped me save money, it still wasn't enough. Earlier in the summer a close friend of mine had broken my laptop and owed me a fair amount of money for it. I would need the money that he owed me in order to go back to Howard.

> "I represented a new generation of those who were steadfast in altering the direction of a nation."

At the time my friend didn't have any money, but he did have a large amount of marijuana, which he offered in compensation for his debt. There was no way that I was going to risk everything I had worked for by going around Omaha selling marijuana to get the money I needed. Even though I wasn't going to sell it, I knew an older family member of mine who could.

I was advised by my mother to reach out to my older cousin informing him about my situation with school. Although he primarily sold crack and cocaine, I was sure he could get rid of the marijuana as well. After calling him, he promised to give me 100 percent of the profit. I wanted to get back to school, and at the time I was willing to do whatever it took to do it.

Parking my car in the alley behind my cousin's house with a large amount of marijuana in my book bag, I got out of the car, walked around the house, and rang the buzzer next to his front door. His porch door was always locked and security cameras were eternally vigilant of every entrance.

I heard, "Who is it," come from inside the front door. While waiting patiently I eyed a watchful camera, which seemed artificial for an otherwise aged house in the middle of the ghetto. I stated my name. Before long my older cousin timidly cracked open the door, and I saw exposed skin that was unnaturally pale from want of never missing a dope sale.

I didn't feel right at that point and knew what I was doing was wrong. In my mind there was no limit to what I would do for a dream that gave my every breath renewed purpose. I didn't feel comfortable asking James, because he had just purchased a laptop for me within the past year. I was going to have to improvise if I wanted to get back to Howard. After all the marijuana was sold, I would finally have enough money, along with what I saved from working to return to school.

Sad to say my mother was still strung out on drugs heavily and after my job was over, I didn't want to go back to Mr. Blake's. My best friend's mother was kind enough to let me stay with them until I left to go back to Howard. With so many obstacles to my success I wondered how far my father had gone to keep his dreams alive.

Before I left to go back to school, I had interviewed with Nebraska's other United States Senator Chuck

Hagel, in hopes of working in his congressional office in Washington, D.C. As soon as I landed in D.C. and as the plane still sat on the runway, my phone rang and it was Chuck Hagel's office. I was notified that I had received the internship and I was ecstatic. I knew that working on the Hill would give me great experience and benefit my resume. Unfortunately, I learned that the internship was unpaid and at the time I couldn't afford to work for free.

Senator Ben Nelson was one of the few Senators that paid interns. I had to notify Chuck Hagel's office that I couldn't take the internship and it was one decision that I deeply regretted. It's an unfortunate fact that many of the most prestigious internships are unpaid because of how competitive they are. The problem is that there are many underprivileged youth who are highly capable but cannot afford to work for free.

Whatever I did, I was going to make sure that my own children wouldn't have to pass up opportunities because they lacked the money to take advantage of them. Fortunately I was offered another position interning for MENTOR, whom I had worked with on different occasions in the past. Mentoring had benefited me greatly, and it was only right to give back.

The first semester of my sophomore year I attempted to balance working, academics, and a social life and did so with lots of trial and error. I spent more time in the library and my experience living back at home again had provided me with the necessary motivation to get back on track. I had to keep pushing.

During a damp early fall morning I met with a photographer on Howard University's yard in the center of the campus as students briskly passed by intent on being on time to class. The noisy sound of tired geese fresh from migratory flight filled the background. After I accepted an opportunity to serve as their scholarship campaign representative for the year, Sallie Mae had sent a photographer to conduct a photo shoot. After posing for marketing materials, I was the subject of a brief interview. I never said no to opportunities, not knowing where the next open door would lead.

Although I had received the American Dream Scholarship, financial aid had again become an issue. Some of the aid that I had been projected to receive had failed to come through, which I had been unprepared for. I needed to get my mother to take out a loan to offset the $30,000 per year tuition at Howard. Since I was legally still a dependent of my mother, I had to get certain documentation from her in order to receive any financial aid.

My mother didn't have a car to get to a fax machine, and I rarely had any luck getting her to sign anything. She was usually somewhere lost in the streets. When I had been younger and needed anything signed for school, even something as simple as a field trip permission form, I had always forged her signature. I knew that if I wanted to get things done, I would have to take a similar approach.

Ean Garrett, American Dream Scholarship recipient, Howard University.

I called my mentor Maggie back home so that she could track down my mother. When I lived back home and she was on hiatus, I'd leave a message for her at her normal hang outs with the hope the messages would get through. When Maggie finally got ahold of the required documentation from my mother, she sent me multiple color copies of everything I needed. That way, anytime I needed financial aid documentation, I could use one of the different copies as if new documents had been sent to me by my mother.

Once again I was forced to forge her signature on any documentation she was required to sign. I also created a fake email account under her name, so that if my school ever had any financial aid questions, I could quickly and efficiently respond. It wasn't something I was proud of, but if I was going to successfully navigate through school it would be necessary.

Somehow I had been lucky enough that year to land a room in the athletes' dorm, which was one of the nicer dorms. Cook Hall had been named after George W. Cook, a Black soldier and later politician who had been elected in 1907 to serve as a Republican in the Sixtieth Congress. The dorm was located in the middle of the campus, which was a gift and a curse. I would frequently mismanage my time thinking I could get to class quickly being in such close proximity, but instead I often ended up getting to class late. Some teachers would go as far as locking the door on students who were tardy. I couldn't blame them, walking in class late disrupted the class, and some teachers would fail to completely regain the students' attention.

During that first semester of my sophomore year at Howard I performed fairly well but with the girl-to-boy ratio, which was 16 to 1, I admit it was difficult not to be distracted. In my English class alone there were thirty-two students and thirty of them were women. Classes with similar gender imbalances were the norm. I often spent study time entertaining women friends of mine. Instead of chasing my dreams I became sidetracked chasing skirts. I found it impossible to feed into what felt natural while pursuing endeavors that were supernatural.

My Aunt Mary Ann once told me, "Not having the inability to control your erotic passions is a sign of mental weakness." She had no idea how profound her words were to me. Heading toward the stars so many Black men that I had known had let their dreams die for the thrill of a ride lasting one night. From afar I could clearly see the traps set for me.

I knew I couldn't afford to be distracted at such a pivotal time in my academic career, especially if I would ever stand atop the peaks of greatness. Yet, it was like the more I focused and put women in my rear view, the more I became aggressively pursued. I knew my father had conceived me while in his early thirties, which was a path of discipline that I wanted to follow.

> "Black men that I had known had let their dreams die for the thrill of a ride lasting one night."

I wanted to race toward my destiny with as little drag as there could possibly be. I would have to make moves that were evasive while sailing in a sea of beautiful faces. I was determined that the next statistical casualty would not be me. And while I kept my mind and body close to me, I guarded the dream that was dearest to me. But it would be through trial and error that I would learn that if I wanted to reach to my full potential I would have to stay mentally strong—meaning that women would have to stay at the bottom of my list of priorities.

Every year when the holidays rolled around, I looked forward to the short vacation like any other college kid. Except this year I wouldn't have much of a home to go to since Tara had moved and my mother lived with Mr. Blake. In the past I would go and visit a friend for Thanksgiving, but for the most part I stayed at school when everyone else left during most breaks, except for Christmas.

When Christmas came, I went home but spent it at my best friend Brandon's house with his family. I had gotten used to spending Christmas away from my mother because I didn't feel like going back to that environment. If I wasn't spending Christmas at my best friend's house, I would go down to Kansas City and spend it with my Aunt Mary Ann as I had previously done.

Aunt Mary continued to provide for me while my mother was still dealing with her own addiction. More than anything, she had become more of a second mother to me. In her eyes my father had been nearly flawless and his passing affected her immensely. I believe she felt she owed it to my father to be there for me in his absence. And I tried to come down and stay with her as much as I could.

The end of the school year came quickly, and this time Upward Bound had offered me a position working as a resident adviser during their summer program again. This time when I came back home, I went straight to my best friend's house and didn't even bother staying at Mr. Blake's. Although I wouldn't stay there, I would always visit Mr. Blake when I had a chance to check on him, even though my mother could hardly ever be found.

This summer was much the same as the last except this time I wasn't taking any summer classes. By the time the end of the summer came, I had saved up a significant amount of money to buy a car. I bought a 1994 BMW

3-Series sedan. The car was located in Missouri, so I had my Aunt Mary Ann go look at the car. She gave the go ahead and I bought it. When I finally got the car, I saw that I had been swindled. The engine wasn't worth the junk yard parts that had been used to rig it.

Still I did my best to fix the car up the best that I could in order to make it into something nice. With the remaining money that I had from my savings, I fixed the car up. I had any dents taken out and repainted the exterior black. I bought chrome rims and new tires. I had the windows tinted dark and put two twelve-inch subwoofers in the trunk.

The inside of the car was reupholstered with a two-tone black-and-tan interior. I also replaced the old headlights with angel eye headlights and replaced the old tail lights with more modern blacked out LEDs. After having some more engine work done, and adding an alarm system, the car looked nearly new. I was finally able to legally obtain the kind of car that I had so much admired in my youth.

At the end of the summer it was time to head back to Howard and surprisingly my car survived the twenty-one-hour drive back to D.C. I had decided to stay off campus this time and found a close-by apartment with one of my friends. For the first time I had to pay for every single one of my bills. I got into the habit early of paying my bills through the semester as soon as I received my refund check, so that if anything happened at least all my bills were paid.

Having my own car at school and my own apartment was a huge distraction and I paid for it. D.C. has a notorious reputation for giving out costly boots and parking tickets. My car was no exception and was getting towed every other week. It also seemed as if I was forced to take it to get serviced more often than I could afford.

People had told me not to get a foreign car but I didn't listen. I was too busy trying to live above my means and was determined to get what at the time I felt I deserved. I should have been patient and waited for it. I also had to deal with the police. I was constantly being pulled over, and I was sure the fact that my car looked like I sold drugs most likely was the cause.

During the first semester of my junior year I started seriously dating a girl I had met while at school. She was petite with a light complexion, jet-black hair, and an infectious smile. She was one of the most beautiful girls I had ever seen. It would be the beginning of a long lasting relationship.

We would discover early that we came from two entirely different backgrounds. Her immediate family alone held degrees from Duke, NYU, Yale, and Harvard. Her father had made a name for himself as an entrepreneur and her mother had previously served in the Clinton Administration. Her parents had laid a strong foundation for their children to have the opportunity to achieve whatever they desired. It was the exact same path that I aspired to travel down while attempting to actualize my own dreams.

As the semester dragged on I had become extremely focused on school. My internship at MENTOR and my involvement with various organizations also kept me busy. The last thing that I needed was something to disrupt my focus. Just when I thought everything was going right, things suddenly took a turn for the worst.

It was late in the evening and the sun had set for a while when some friends and I headed out. I had called for the front passenger position and was surprised when no one else put up a fight. It was a decision that I would later regret. We were headed out for the night, just me and a few of the guys I had become friends with over the past few years at Howard. When we pulled off, it seemed as if it would be a regular night out. It wouldn't take long before I would find out otherwise.

We had been driving less than five minutes when blue and red lights were flashing behind us. My friend who had been driving started to panic and told us that he didn't have any insurance—and also had a warrant out for his arrest. Thinking that I would simply get a ticket that he could later reimburse me for, and not wanting so see any of us go to jail, we switched seats. I still can't imagine how with the search light focused on us they didn't see me unbuckle my seatbelt and hop into the driver's seat, as my friend slid into the passenger's side.

After less than a minute, two Black female police officers walked up to the driver's side window and asked for my driver's license, registration, and proof of insurance. She took all of the documentation and made her way back to the police cruiser. I felt pretty confident I would be fine being that I had no warrants for my arrest. After what seemed like hours, the police officer got out of her cruiser and returned to the driver's side window asking me to step out of the car.

Confused, we all asked what the problem was. She responded by sternly informing me that I was being arrested for driving an unregistered vehicle. Not thinking that I would be arrested, my friend tried to explain to the officer that we had switched seats, he had actually been driving, and that the car belonged to him. Nothing we said changed her mind.

As I stepped out of the car, traffic curiously crept by on New York Avenue, one of the busiest streets in Washington, D.C. The officer walked me to the rear of the vehicle and ordered me to put my hands on top of the trunk as she patted me down. Before I knew it, I was having my hands put behind my back and handcuffed.

As I sat in the back of the police cruiser, I had a flashback to when I was a seven-year-old misguided product of the ghetto facing similar circumstances. The trip to the police station was one I would never forget. I was exactly in a place that I said I'd never again see, and directly furthering stereotypes that predicted that I had reached the epitome of my destiny. Before I knew it, I was sitting in a holding cell waiting for my friends to come and post my bond.

As I sat on the cold and hard metal bench, I attempted to mentally drown out the irate inmate in the cell next to me. I tried not to think about how this could possibly affect my future. My mission was to help my family and give back by helping as many people as I could along the way. Yet, for some reason there seemed to be one barrier after another.

> "Before I knew it, I was having my hands put behind my back and handcuffed."

I stared past the iron bars in front of me through a small window high up on the wall. Through the window I could see the faint glimmer of stars in the night sky. Just as my quest to land among the glistening points of light had grown dim, I found strength from my dreams within.

After a few hours, I was released from jail with a newfound appreciation for my own freedom. Those two hours in a holding cell were enough time to get it embedded in my brain that I would never sit behind bars again. I paid a fine and was lucky enough not to get charged with the misdemeanor, although the fact that I was arrested would never be erased from my record. And just when I thought I had hit rock bottom, I soon discovered that rock bottom was merely the shallow waters of a bottomless abyss.

Toward the end of my first semester and close to finals, I received a call from my mother. She informed me that my sister had been in a life-threatening car accident. My sister drove a blue two-door Saturn Ion. She had been driving when she slid off the road after hitting a patch of ice. Her small car had been totaled after it had wrapped around a tree like a crushed soda can. The rescue squad had been forced to use the "jaws of life" to free her from the wreckage of crushed metal. Her airbags had also failed to deploy. Luckily she had dropped my niece off at her babysitter's right before the accident occurred.

Tara had already been in a coma for eight days before her dad had contacted me and my mother. In case my sister didn't make it, it was clear that her father wanted to ensure that he obtained custody over my niece. Her father and our mother had never gotten along after their divorce. My sister was paralyzed from the waist down with significant trauma to her brain.

I remember the first time we had a conversation after the accident. After she had awakened from her coma, I finally heard the sound of her fragile voice and I completely broke down. She had always been my heart. She reminded me that I had to be strong because everyone in the family had invested their hopes in me. I knew that she was right and that my success encompassed so much more than my own well-being.

My ambition had become beyond fatigued, and I had reached the bottom of an emotional abyss. But I remembered how many bottomless pits I had defiantly emerged from before. And I couldn't afford to drop the ball in my hands if somehow I was going to successfully do it all again.

The second semester of my junior year came and I was already looking forward to the summer. My internship at MENTOR had been going well, and I had been invited to serve as a liaison on behalf of the organization at a taping of the *Oprah* TV show. The taping of the show would be dedicated to various organizations and individuals who were making a real impact through mentoring. I had never taken the time to watch a full episode of *Oprah*, but I still found all that she had achieved to be personally inspiring.

We arrived at Harpo Studios in Chicago on a wet and chilly day in early March. I was accompanied by Tonya Wiley, who then served as the Senior Vice President at MENTOR. Tonya was short, with a rich brown skin tone and a sincere demeanor. Throughout the years she had been highly supportive of all my endeavors, and I was glad she had been selected to accompany me.

We attempted to keep ourselves warm as we stood outside the entrance to the studio, along with a growing crowd of impatient fellow audience members. In the center of the crowd, I looked around us and noticed that the composition of the audience was comprised almost entirely of middle-aged white women. It was clear that Oprah had acquired the same ability to bridge racial divides that my father once possessed. It was a quality that I admired in them both and forever longed to imbed deep within my character.

When we had finally taken our seats in a reserved section, we found that it was full of special guests who, similar to us, were present on behalf of their organizations. The one commonality that had come to unite us all was our heavy involvement in mentoring. Not long after we had taken our seats, the taping of the show began.

After being on set for some time our section was exclusively allowed to go on stage and meet Oprah. Her face was confident, and I could easily sense the drive and sense of purpose pouring from her soul. After exchanging a few words, which expressed my admiration for her work, Oprah stood between Tonya and me as we posed for pictures. Meeting her reminded me of how much more I wanted to achieve, and it was extremely beneficial to see a woman who shared my African American heritage and had accomplished so much in one lifetime.

After the taping of the show we were invited to socialize with some of the other special guests at a small gathering outside of the studio at a hotel. Susan Taylor, the former editor-in-chief of *Essence* magazine, was entertaining a small number of guests when I noticed Hill Harper in a corner enjoying an hors d'oeuvre or two. Hill Harper was at the top of his game, as he currently was an actor on the prime time television show *CSI: New York*, held two graduate degrees from Harvard, and had recently published a book.

I congratulated him on his new book, *Letters to a Young Brother*, along with his work with mentoring. I knew that he had attended Harvard Law School in his early days, and I had made up my mind to continue following my father's path by also attending law school upon graduation. Particularly, I was interested in his technique for preparing for the law school admission exam or the LSAT.

After asking him what his technique was for taking the LSAT, he responded by saying, "Take every practice test that you can get your hands on." I was determined to do just that. It seemed like an arduous task, but I was prepared to circle the earth twice if that's what it was going to take to keep my dreams alive.

The author with former editor-in-chief of Essence *magazine, Susan Taylor (center), and MENTOR/National Mentoring Partnership Senior Vice-President Tonya Wiley (right).*

The summer of 2007 would be the most important summer for me yet. It would be time to submit my law school applications during the fall of my senior year. This meant that not only would they not receive my grades from the beginning of my senior year, but I had one more summer to add something special to my resume. Luckily, James had a contact at a large law firm in D.C. After applying for a position as a paralegal intern at the firm, I received the position.

That summer I worked over fifty hours a week at the firm, while also taking an LSAT review course in preparation for the law school entrance exam. In addition to my already existing obligations, I accepted a position as the President of the Howard University chapter of Students for Barack Obama. At that point I still had a partiality to politics and was sure it would be a great experience.

The author (left) getting schooled by best-selling author and CSI: New York *actor Hill Harper at private reception following a taping of the* Oprah *show.*

Leading up to the 2008 Presidential election, the country had already been experiencing tell-tale signs of the economic debacle and ideological divisiveness soon to come. I thought the experience would give me a priceless insight into the question of whether our political system was still capable of creating the change the general population cried for. I wanted to play a part in history by being directly involved in the process of helping to get then-Senator Obama elected.

The quality of my work at the law firm suffered tremendously. While at work I took practice LSAT exams and orchestrated a rally for Obama during the Democratic Presidential Debate, which would be held at Howard later that summer. I began to miss deadlines at work and my boss was constantly on my case. My study efforts for the LSAT also failed to be fully productive with everything that I was involved in. I had been given all of the opportunities that I had asked for, but had not yet discovered a way to organize each responsibility, while still excelling in each task and maximizing my full potential.

The day of the Democratic Presidential Debate at Howard University had finally come. The sun was out and not a cloud could be seen across the afternoon sky. For the past few months, I had tirelessly contacted individuals all throughout the tri-state area in an attempt to rally as many supporters as possible for a pre-debate event. We congregated on the north side of the university campus near the entrance, just a few hours before the debate was scheduled to begin. Supporters from all opposing campaigns were busy setting up on opposing sides of Georgia Avenue, which ran parallel to the west side of Howard's campus.

Obama signs and paraphernalia were all around me as I took a deep breath trying to soak it all in. The feeling was overwhelming to see something that I had worked so hard for successfully executed. Most of the people who had come to show support were students and young professionals. In the midst of the crowd chanting "Obama 08," two black SUVs discreetly pulled up to the curb in front of the crowd.

> "I whispered in Barack Obama's ear,
> 'We're all watching.'"

I tried to hide any sign that I knew what was about to unfold as perplexed faces all stared at the vehicles. The rear passenger door of the second SUV opened, and excitement overtook the crowd as Senator Obama stepped out of the back seat of the vehicle. A friend of mine, Brandon Neal, who had close connections within the campaign, had been able to help orchestrate the appearance. After Senator Obama addressed the crowd while surrounded by droves of secret service agents, Brandon introduced me to the man himself. As we shook hands and engaged in a short dialogue, the last thing I whispered in Barack Obama's ear was, "We're all watching."

As a Black male in America, I directly had a stake in the outcome of the election. Not because I wanted someone who looks like me to win, but simply because his fate was intertwined with that of every other Black male in America who had a diligent work ethic, credentials to match, and the type of ambition to reach for the best that America had to offer. At that point in time I had the ambition, but I needed to work on obtaining the consistent work ethic to match it.

The author hosts then-Senator Barack Obama (left) shortly before the 2008 Democratic Presidential Debate, held at Howard University in Washington, D.C.

Back at my internship, my last week had come before I knew it. While working on compiling a few binders in preparation for an upcoming administrative hearing, I was called into the human resources office. I began to prepare myself for the worst.

As I walked into the office, the same woman who had hired me informed me that I would not be asked to return to work the next summer. She cast doubt about my future potential to attend law school and suggested that finding work on Capitol Hill may suit me better. I had a feeling that possibly my lackluster performance and publicized work within the Obama campaign had a part to play in her conclusions.

I wouldn't allow her remarks to stifle my dreams; if anything it fueled my ambition and motivation to prove that she was wrong. At the same time the news wasn't a shock to me because I knew that I didn't deserve it. I had a habit of trying to juggle too many things at one time, instead of focusing on the task at hand and putting all of my energy into what was before me.

I deeply regretted disappointing James, because that he had stuck his neck out for me. It was a wake-up call that I urgently needed if I was ever going to grow. I would make sure that next time I would make better use of any opportunity that I had been given.

Senior year came faster than I ever could have imagined. I often had thoughts about college when I was younger but never had the slightest idea that I would make it this far. Now it was time to ensure that I would make it one step further. I moved in with three friends in a four-bedroom row-house in a rough part of town. It was time to think about my future after Howard.

Since my LSAT studies had not been very productive during the summer, I did everything I could to make up for lost time. I continued to work hard in class, and following Hill Harper's advice I dedicated every waking hour to taking as many practice law school entrance exams as I could find. I also spent a good portion of my time applying to law schools all over the country.

Just in case I didn't get into law school, I contemplated alternative positions within the military and CIA. I was determined to exhaust every option. Although figuring out where my future lay took up most of my thoughts, there were still a few other hurdles that I would have to bypass first.

On a Friday night, during our school's homecoming, an organization that I belonged to was hosting a party at a local night club. I picked up one of my close friends, and when we arrived, we discovered that there was no parking anywhere within a fifteen-minute walk to the club. We eventually ended up finding a parking spot that was pretty far away and in what I felt was a shady neighborhood.

There were no houses on either side of the block, and not many streetlights, but we were tired of looking for parking and ready to go inside the night club. I finally parked the car and then set my alarm system. My alarm system came with a pager, so that if anyone touched my car, it would notify me. With my alarm system on, I felt reassured about where I had parked my car, and we made our way to the club.

The night club started to die down around two o'clock, and we were ready to leave. We began making the long fifteen-minute trek back to my car. When we were around the corner from where my car was parked, the quiet became deafening, and something just didn't seem right. The block was full of trees whose shadows made the night a deeper black. As we approached the corner, we noticed a dark hooded figure nervously fidgeting below a street light on the corner. He moved as if he were looking out for something he hoped would never come.

My friend reached his arm across my chest and stopped me before I could take another step. The dark figure must have heard our approach as it turned around and stared back at us with equal caution. My instincts forced my body to surge with adrenaline, and my heartbeat started to increase rapidly. As we proceeded with all awareness toward the corner, our eyes followed the nervous figure as he walked off to our right into the distance.

When we looked left, back in the direction of my car, to both of our surprise my car was being broken into. The nervous hooded figure must have been the lookout and had tipped off his friends before making his escape into the night. It was my guess that I had been too far away from the car for the alarm system to successfully have paged me. I'm sure that since the club didn't shut down for another few hours, they weren't expecting us to return so soon.

About five or six Black males, most appearing slightly older or younger than I, looked back at us with emotionless faces. They slowly retreated into the shadows with their stolen treasures. We were clearly outnumbered and defenseless, but with my car looking like I sold drugs, I'm sure they only retreated as a precaution. Had they known for a fact that neither of us was armed, I'm sure the outcome would've been a lot different.

When we reached the car, I saw that they had taken my subwoofer out of my trunk. They had also ripped my stereo out of the dashboard, and made off with a few sets of brand new sneakers along with other articles of clothing from the trunk. When we initially approached them, they had also been in the process of taking off my rims and intended to leave my car sitting on a pile of bricks. I had wheel locks on my rims that needed a key to unlock for this exact reason, but they could be busted off if hit with enough force. My wheel locks must have held them up until now.

I walked up to the car, closed the trunk, and left the scattered papers and trash lying on the concrete. The silent figures watched from the next corner while standing next to a running car with its headlights off. I knew that with so many people the likelihood that at least one of them had a gun was pretty high, especially when doing something dangerous like stripping down cars. I jumped in the car and my friend quickly got in on the passenger's side. I put the transmission into drive and tried to pull off. The car only jerked slightly and stood still as the engine revved. They must have partially taken one of the rims off.

I got out of the car and looked at all the rims. I could see that they had been halfway successful in taking off my front passenger's side tire. I took a second to think. Now that they knew the car was mine, they could take my keys and just steal the whole car, or they could get us for all the jewelry and cash we had on us.

As we contemplated our next move, the silent figures crammed into the car at the opposite end of the street and began slowly heading in our direction. My friend exited the car and we walked back in the direction that we had come. The car continued to creep in our direction, still with its headlights off. As we turned the corner about half a block away from where my car was parked, they continued to follow us. I remember that there was a building about two blocks away that always had police cars in front of it, so we decided to head there. We began to jog.

The car following us sped up and screeched to a halt at the end of the corner that we had just left. As soon as we saw the car roll down its tinted windows, we began to sprint. The same time that we began to run, we saw the car speed off in another direction. We had no idea if they were trying to cut us off or not. I thought about cutting through some houses, but now we were less than a block away from where I had seen the police cars. We decided to take our chances. Breathing heavily we finally reached the building. After knocking on the door for what seemed like a lifetime, a police officer eventually came to the door.

We were lucky that my friend had AAA service, which we could use to put my tire back on the car. The police took us back to where my car sat and waited with us until the AAA tow truck arrived. The police officer tried to persuade me to file a police report, but where I was from, you never filed police reports. Instead, I just accepted it as a loss. After the tow truck driver put the tire back on the car, I dropped my friend off and headed home.

Everything that had happened was my fault, because I should have seen it. My car had been too flashy to bring to D.C. and attracted the type of negative attention I had always tried to stray away from. Where I grew up, I never would have parked my car on a conspicuous block. In a seemingly safe college environment my street instincts had become too lax, and in certain environments you can't afford to ever relax. You have to be constantly aware of your surroundings at all times. I recalled the conversation that I had with my gang-affiliated friend Deon almost fourteen years earlier.

I knew in the future that I would never have a car with rims again, and next time I'd invest in something a lot less conspicuous. It had been immature and foolish to spend money getting them in the first place. After that, I was ready to get rid of the car, which started having mechanical problems anyway. I eventually sold the car a few months later and promised myself that after what happed, I would learn from the experience and mature.

That fall I had been spending countless time and an immense amount of energy applying to various law schools. Due to my mother's meager financial position, all application fees were waived. As a result I tried to make the most of having my application fees waived by applying to as many law schools as I possibly could. When I would finish applying, I would have completed applications for a total of twenty-seven different schools around the country.

The diversity of the schools ranged from long-shot schools like Harvard and Columbia to safer schools where my chances of getting in were presumably higher. If I wasn't preparing for the law school admissions exam, I was going to one of my seven classes that semester or filling out law school applications. With a full course load I was taking twenty-one credits that semester and would have to take twenty-three credits the next semester in order to graduate in four years.

It became the norm around the country to graduate in five years. After talking to James he told me, "There's no reason you shouldn't graduate in four years." It was just the type of motivation I needed. I didn't have a year to waste. Tomorrow wasn't promised. If my dreams were going to stay alive, I needed not only to pass every class to graduate in four years, but I still needed to take the law school entrance exam as well.

December came and it was time for me to take the LSAT. I was studying no less than eight hours a day in preparation for it. I had studied tirelessly and was content that I had done everything that I could in order to maximize my chances of doing well. Some even said I was studying too much. I was also nervous because I had never been the best multiple-choice test-taker growing up. I was going to give it all I had nonetheless.

The day of the exam I woke up early. I tried to eat a hearty meal and felt I was as ready to take the test as I would ever be. My testing site was Catholic University. After arriving at the testing site, I noticed that there were only two other Blacks taking the exam in a field of white faces.

I wondered what it had been like when my father had taken the law school entrance exam back in the early 1970s. With the thought of my father being in the same position forty years earlier, I became empowered. Our proctor handed out the exam, and I reminded myself that I couldn't have studied any more than I had. During the three-hour exam I pushed myself through it thwarting fatigue. After the exam was over all I could do was leave it up to fate. I had come too far for the ride to end prematurely.

The last semester of my senior year would prove to be pivotal in my quest to live out my father's dream. When my law school entrance exam came back, my score was disappointing. I had no idea what I had done wrong. I studied harder than I had ever studied for anything. I had even followed Hill Harper's advice by taking as many practice exams as I possibly could.

As my dreams became dim, my options had also dwindled. I could either wait and take the LSAT again, or I could take my chances and use the scores that I already had. I didn't want to wait a whole year again to reapply to law school. Honestly, I had felt that I had given my all when I took the exam the first time. Multiple-choice exams had never been my strong area. Regardless, I had faith that when the cards fell I would get dealt the hand that I was meant to have.

On the eve of Cinco de Mayo, as I left a bar with my girlfriend and another group of close friends, I received an unexpected phone call. After hearing a monotone voice of a woman who was calling from a strange number, I immediately realized who it was. The woman never told me her name, but she did inform me that she was a field agent for the CIA and I was being interviewed. I slipped into the shade of a dark shadow and immediately was reminded of a Matt Damon scene from the movie *The Good Shepherd*.

I started to regret the few Coronas that I had consumed and was sure that the awkward timing of the call was part of the interview strategy. After holding a conversation for what seemed like a short amount of time, I could sense that my concept of time was flawed, as my friends who were driving became impatient as they waited for me. By the end of my conversation with the anonymous woman, I began to have reservations about living such a life of obscurity and secrecy. I doubted that any attempt to embark upon that career path would likely fit my ultimate ambitions or ideology. Nevertheless it was an option to be considered.

In the meanwhile, every day after coming home from work or school, I would check the mail for correspondence from any of the law schools that I had applied to. Unfortunately it didn't take long for the rejection letters to pile up. I started to think about the possibility of not getting into law school at all. I started to doubt myself and wonder whether I had what it would take to actualize my dreams.

Although I had applied to the CIA as a secondary plan, I dreaded having to put law school off while working a job that I felt would be an unnecessary detour from a path that I was steadfast on taking. I was even ready to take the law school admissions exam again and repetitiously endure the overall admissions process for a second time. But in my mind one year lost would be one more year that my family would have to continue to endure struggle. It was a detour that I prayed I would never have to make. Yet, waiting another year to reapply to law school was a realistic possibility that I had no choice but to seriously consider.

In the late spring, I still had not received any acceptance letters from a single law school. It seemed to be evident that my LSAT score was the one thing holding me back. After a while I had been rejected by every school except Harvard Law, Catholic Law, and Nebraska Law. Eventually, I received a notification from Harvard that I had not been accepted. I was devastated as Harvard had been my number one choice. I was still resolute not to give up hope. After all I still had two law schools to hear from.

Before long I received a letter from Catholic University notifying me that I had been placed on a waiting list, in case any seats in the upcoming class opened up. The news was bittersweet and failed to bring me much comfort. In the meantime I struggled to stay optimistic.

I had reached a point where I was ready to accept that I wouldn't be following my father's footsteps, when I received a call from James. He informed me that I had some mail at his house, which I used as an alternate address while in school. When he finally arrived at my house, he walked in the door and handed me the envelope, sat down on my sofa, and curiously waited for me to open it. It was from the University of Nebraska College of Law, which was a school I almost had not applied to. It was the last college that I needed to hear from.

As I ran my fingers across the envelope, I thought it was ironic that I even applied to any schools from back home, since I had refused to do so when I had applied to undergraduate colleges in high school. I thought back to the moment that I had nervously eyed my admission letter from Howard four years earlier. After more prodding by James I finally opened the envelope. I was accepted! With a full tuition scholarship.

Before I fully internalized my acceptance, I was forced to decide whether to attend law school now or to work a year and reapply with hopes of getting into a better school. Although Nebraska's law school was a tier one school, it had not been any of the top twenty-five that I had set my heart on. Still, I felt like an athlete seeking the quickest way to escape an unfavorable situation, who couldn't risk tearing any ligaments by putting off the pros by waiting another year in college. Like them, I feared putting off my dreams, knowing that there was a possibility that the unpredictability of time could keep me from reaching them.

Furthermore, I thought about the more extensive support system I would have back in my home state. I also had thoughts of reconnecting with my mother and making up for lost time; at least I had hoped it would happen that way. Either way it felt like the whole world had just been lifted off my shoulders. I decided I was going back home for law school.

> "I feared putting off my dreams, knowing that there was a possibility that the unpredictability of time could keep me from reaching them."

Just when I thought that my dreams were dead, somehow I was able to squeak through. I knew that if my work ethic had been more thorough all four years, and not just sporadically excellent, that this process would have been a lot easier. The difficulties I faced with my internship at the law firm the previous summer and the law school entrance process deeply humbled me. The dream that I shared with my father still had a beating heart. My bachelor's degree wasn't a big enough barrier for me from poverty. I had to keep going. Although I felt as if I had aimed for the stars and missed, I had been given a second chance and I was going to make the most of it.

◦◦

Standing behind the velvet curtain, I could hear the crowd start to become restless as a rising chatter fell upon the stage like waves crashing against jagged rocks on some far away shore. It was April 1 of my senior year, and we were back stage at the historic Lincoln Theater in Washington, D.C. While peeking from behind the curtain onto the stage I imagined Duke Ellington leading his band in one of his latest jazz compositions. I could picture Louis Armstrong with full cheeks blowing air into a trumpet as it escaped in the form of rhythmic melodies. I could almost hear the voice of Billie Holiday filling the theater with her soulful sounds. I then took a moment to pay homage to the pioneers who had once graced the stage before me.

The theater continued to host history as I patiently waited backstage while making small talk with Senator John Kerry and The Reverend Jesse Jackson. The event entitled "Our America" was hosted by MTV's "Sway," and I had been asked to join a few other young people to speak about issues affecting our America—or America as seen as through our limited perspectives.

Reverend Jackson was the first to address the crowd. He began with his notorious chant, "I am somebody." Before long the crowd was repeating his words full of self-inspiration, and the thunder of an auditorium filled with fired up youth shook the stage beneath me. I felt remorse for Senator Kerry as he walked out on stage, knowing that Reverend Jackson's energy would make him a hard act to follow.

As I stood backstage going over my speech and making last-minute revisions, John Kerry's speech lasted shorter than I had expected, and it would soon be my turn to address the large crowd. Out of the assortment of young guest speakers, I had the most public speaking experience, and as a result had been scheduled to speak last. Sensing nervousness from the others, I gave words of encouragement and wished them well as one after another was called to the stage.

It seemed as if only seconds had passed when I looked around me only to see the stage manager running back and forth frantically. I ignored the frenzy around me and focused. At that moment I prayed as I always did before any speech and imagined my father standing next to me.

I had given speeches before, but this one was particularly special. It would be the largest gathering of my peers that I had ever addressed. Speaking to large crowds full of adults who were satisfactorily patting their stomachs after devouring three-course meals was easy. Addressing a mass group of my own peers, who often tend to be one's harshest critics, was entirely different.

Nonetheless I longed to seize the moment. The crowd was comprised of at-risk youth, many who share similar stories, and more importantly would be able to empathize with a dream I held onto. They too were forgotten. I saw it as an opportunity to share my father's dream and to speak on issues that had constantly been eating away at my mind. I shook my limbs to loosen up and was as focused as I had ever been when I heard Sway call my name. I then walked on stage.

As I became blinded by the bright lights, the audience appeared like nothing more than a shadow whose applause was a stark reminder of their presence. After standing behind the podium and taking a deep breath, I began:

> *Tonight, I ask you not to view me as an advocate blindly speaking on issues which I know nothing about. Tonight, I come to you as a young man who has personally braved the trenches and has seen first-hand how poverty is shaking the foundations of this nation. I've seen drugs, prostitution, gangs, and violence all destroy my community. I know that poverty not only affects the larger cities in America, but as a native of Omaha, Nebraska, I know that poverty is in every corner of this nation ... my story serves as a true testament to the ideals of America."*

My birthday usually always landed the week before finals. An envelope arrived in the mail and the return address was that of my mother. I wondered what it could be. She had failed to support me mentally, physically, or monetarily in any way since I had first arrived at Howard almost four years earlier. She had not the slightest idea how I was living due to the fact that she had never visited once before to see for herself.

As I opened up the envelope, I pulled out a birthday card, and twenty-five dollars slid out of the inside of the card into my lap. I understood it as a timid effort at reconciliation. I readily accepted her silent attempt at redemption. Still dealing with her addiction, I knew the evil that she was battling day in and day out. I had always embraced her—flaws and all. When family and friends fall down, you never abandon them, rather you provide support to help them rebound. I started to think that fate had sent me back home to Nebraska for more reasons than one.

9

Landing on the Moon

With a burning fire underneath I released my grief into
  a forgetful ocean, as I headed towards the constellations
  carried by spacecraft propulsion.

Passing uneventfully through the thinning atmosphere, my sigh
  of relief was brief knowing somehow I had to conserve air.

As the cockpit caught ablaze I pondered if it had all been
  worth it; still intent on my purpose, I braced for impact
  with the lunar surface.

Stepping onto the celestial body I regretted that I had failed
  to touch the stars; yet the satellite was the perfect stepping
  stone to colonize Mars.

ℰℒ

Getting back home was a challenge. After paying all of my bills I didn't have any money left, but I still had to find a way. I decided that the best thing to do would be to sell my furniture and if necessary a few personal items. After about a week I sold everything and had just enough money for a plane ticket and to ship some boxes home.

Moving back to Nebraska was bittersweet. The sweet part was that I looked forward to seeing all my friends again and to having the opportunity to foster old relationships. I also looked forward to spending time with my mother. For the first time in years she was clean again. And now that she was clean from drugs, maybe we would be able to make up for lost time.

The bitter part about going to school back home was the location of the law college. The University of Nebraska was located in a smaller town called Lincoln, which also served as the state capital some sixty miles from Omaha. I was fortunate enough to find an apartment directly across the street from the law school. The apartment's location was especially critical because at the time I still didn't have a car. An old friend of mine whom I would be rooming with had found the apartment, which was quite modest to say the least.

After selling all of my furniture, the only things I possessed were boxes of clothing and an air mattress that I had purchased to sleep on. At the time I didn't care that I hardly had anything to my name. The simple fact that I was in law school was all that mattered. I was willing to starve now banking on the odds that I would one day feast later.

New student orientation was held at the law college at the end of August. When I walked into a cool air conditioned building, gladly escaping the August heat, I saw a crowd of people bustling back and forth from various tables hosting attractive displays. I walked forward down a wide hall and suspiciously eyed what would become my home away from home for the next three years.

It became readily apparent to me, as I followed signs while navigating the building, that there were very few people who resembled my ethnicity. Rather than talk much, my demeanor was reserved. After I started to become aware of how tense everyone looked, I began to wonder what I had gotten myself into.

The first few months of law school were tough. Initially, it was an extremely large culture shock. Coming from Howard University, a historically Black institution where almost all of my classes were completely full of Black students, to a setting where I was the only Black student in almost every class was difficult. I admit the transition was hard to deal with at first.

Many of my classmates had never had a friend who was Black, and from my own perspective I had never been around so many whites in my life. Most schools I had attended, from elementary school through college, had a minority population that made up a fair cross-section of the student body. The color of my skin would now become a constantly distracting thought. I knew that every time I opened my mouth to comment on a hypothetical question or to answer any other question when called upon that I was representing my entire race. The pressure could become unbearable at times.

All my life I never had any issues making friends, but that would dramatically change. At first I didn't have many friends at the law school, which made it even tougher to get help studying or to get notes if I missed class. In most classes I sat alone and after class proceeded to go straight home.

The coursework was rigorous. I had never been given so much work to do at any other time during my previous academic experiences. At Howard, I was used to studying what I had thought was a significant amount, but now I studied around the clock. I rarely had any free time.

I had decided not to get cable so that I could focus. I didn't have much down time, but I made sure that I made time to read leisurely in between reading for classes. Reading fiction between my reading assignments and various projects became my escape.

Scholastically, the first year became an experiment regarding my study habits. Most of my classmates took in-class notes on a laptop computer. My own laptop, which my mentor James had bought for me when I first arrived at Howard, was too delicate to bring to class. The screen of the laptop was broken. I had to improvise by using a library book end to keep my laptop screen from falling backwards.

I was too embarrassed to take my laptop to class, so instead I took notes by hand. This method of note taking proved to be useless, as the teacher often spoke faster than my writing speed would allow me to keep up with. Also my handwriting was so bad that often while reviewing my notes I was unable to read my own manuscript.

I was also socially depressed. I found few students to genuinely connect with, whether they were Black, white, or any other race for that matter. The law school was also isolated on a separate part of the campus, which made it hard to mingle or network with other graduate students at the university. I did have a few old high school friends who were still in the undergraduate program at the university, but they couldn't relate to my new lifestyle dedicated solely to studying.

I heard rumors from sources back home that some people thought I had changed as a result of going to Howard and now as a law student. I didn't let the rumors get to me. If anything I noticed that my Black peers treated me differently. As an educated Black who came from an environment where few were educated, I could imagine how I could easily have been labeled. What they had failed to realize was that everything I did was for them.

I wanted to show my peers that you didn't have to sell crack, step on a stage and rap, or catch a ball on the field while entertaining others, simultaneously risking

life-altering injuries to make it out of the ghetto. I
aspired to reach a place where I could help my people
collectively defy the recurring cycles of poverty. In the
end they would see the master blueprint.

I rarely went outside of the house in order to avoid the
long gazes and quiet whispers. When inside the house I
often was alone because my roommate was hardly ever
home. I was still having trouble coming to terms with
the reality that I would have to sacrifice my happiness,
friendships, and three years out of my life for a dream.

> "I would have to sacrifice my happiness,
> friendships, and three years out of my life
> for a dream."

There is a saying in law school that I learned from
my legal writing professor. He said, "Being a lawyer
means never being able to relax." If that was the case
it proved to be even more so for me. Since I had barely
made it into law school, even if I wasn't studying, all I
could think about was doing well so that I could stay
in law school. Our school didn't have the best record of
keeping Black students from flunking out and I didn't
want to be one of them.

It was November 4, 2008. I had briefly taken a break
from my studies and headed to Omaha to meet up
with Aunt Mary Ann at my Aunt Gertrude's house. I
sat next to my Aunt Mary Ann who was in her early

fifties and my Great Aunt Gertrude who was well into her seventies. Each of us represented three different generations with our own American experience, but today's Presidential election was monumental for us all. With the lights low, the glow of the television filled the room. As we watched the television intensely the votes of each state began to come in.

When all of the votes had finally been counted from every state, Barack Obama had gained 365 electoral votes to John McCain's 173 and had been announced as the next President of the United States. Tears rolled down my Aunt Gertrude's eyes as America had elected its first African American President in its 232-year history. She had never thought that she would live to see a Black President in her lifetime.

It was a gorgeous sight to see that against insurmountable odds he had prevailed. I was just proud to have played a small role in helping him to realize his ambitions, because I knew exactly what it felt like to have a dream. And I was still in hot pursuit of my own.

The end of my first semester finally rolled around. Many law schools wouldn't test students until the end of the entire first year, but our school tested first-year law school students in each class at the end of the first semester. This was due to law firm requests for some way to gauge how well students were doing in comparison to each other, so that they could choose summer associates for the summer following our first year. I was extremely nervous with finals around the corner. I saw so many students studying in groups and had not been invited to study with any of them.

Since we were only tested at the end of the semester, the only way to retain the information was to compress it all into an outline. When I finally started to create an outline for my classes in preparation for finals, my notes were in disarray. Large amounts of time had been wasted by typing up my handwritten notes, which in many cases were not legible.

There were many concepts that I had yet to grasp, and I dreaded approaching my professors for help, so that they could sternly suggest that maybe law school wasn't for me. I didn't want to be the stereotypical Black student who couldn't make the cut. The few things that gave me strength at that point were the fact that I knew my father had gotten through law school and the knowledge that my family was depending on me.

I stayed in the library during the day and at my dining room table at night. Failure tends to make the perfect fire to motivate, and I was intent not to fail. I imagined that my roommate thought I was insane every time he walked through the door and discovered me studying in the same exact spot.

If I didn't do well, I was determined for it not to be because I hadn't worked hard enough. The night before finals began, papers and empty cans of energy drinks were scattered across my dining room table. Feeling that I had nothing else to give, I went to bed and was ready for whatever fate awaited me.

Shortly after Christmas break we received our grades. Instead of actual number or letter grades we were put into percentage quartiles based upon our performance in each class. These grades were extremely important because they were a deciding factor as to whether or not we would have a shot at becoming a summer associate for a number of local law firms. I opened a plain envelope and held my breath as I looked at my grades.

My grades were dismal. I had scored in the bottom percentile of almost every class. I came to the conclusion that there must have been something wrong with me. Maybe I had a learning disability, or maybe I wasn't smart enough to be in law school in the first place.

I was reminded of my first few weeks during the Junior Statesmen Program at Georgetown. During that tough time, I also initially lacked the confidence to academically compete with my white counterparts. I knew law school wouldn't be easy, but I hadn't expected to have as hard a time as I did. Either way something had to change or I would flunk out of law school entirely, which was the thing I feared most.

At the beginning of the next semester one of my professors had asked to meet with me. I was almost sure it was because of my poor performance in his class. He happened to be one of the professors who intimidated me the most. He taught the subject of civil procedure, one of the hardest first-year subjects. He was tall with white hair and had a voice that made everything he said sound like the butt of a joke.

During the meeting he brought up my low test scores and feared that I would fail his class if I didn't turn around. He noticed that I sat alone in class and wondered what other factors might be responsible for my poor performance. I disclosed certain factors such as the culture shock, taking notes by hand, and even the fact that he personally intimidated me. He seemed to understand. Just talking about my issues seemed to relieve a lot of the stress that I had been having prior to our meeting. He gave me encouragement and after the meeting I felt a lot better, and hope crept back into my distraught spirit.

I completely changed the way I studied and dedicated all of my time to learning the course materials. A major addition to my more efficient study habits came from a new laptop that I had purchased. I found that I could type much faster than I could write and my organization and note taking abilities became exceptionally more efficient. I also forced myself to get over the intimidation of my professors and met with all of them on different occasions throughout my second semester.

I was also more aggressive when it came to finding study partners and found that it helped tremendously to bounce concepts off one another. I felt more comfortable in my classes and better about law school in general.

When the time of year came for first-year students to interview with law firms for summer associate positions, I didn't even try. With my grades it would be a waste of my time and theirs. I didn't know what I was going to do during the summer to gain legal experience and income, but since there was still a fair amount of time before the end of the school year, I still had some time to figure it out.

When I came to law school I seldom left the house, so I was sure I wouldn't get into any trouble. I knew how important it was for my future to keep clear of any legal problems. As result I constantly was going out of my way to keep my nose clean. Unfortunately, I would come to find out that regardless of my caution, trouble just seemed to follow me wherever I went.

On a Friday night, I made the forty-five-minute drive to Omaha with my roommate and headed to a local night club with a couple of other friends. My best friend at the time was driving his car and had parked next to the establishment. The club was located in a somewhat bad part of town, not too far from where I had grown up. Ironically, it was across the street from where my father's law firm had been located. I always eyed the building whenever I passed it by thinking of him.

In Lincoln, I had a few friends, but it was nice to go to Omaha and hang around old friends every once in a while. That night the club didn't prove to be as entertaining as we had hoped so we decided to leave early. As we approached the car, we noticed two police officers standing next to it. When we finally got close enough, they asked who the car belonged to. My best friend said it was his car. The officer then proceeded to inform him that he had parked on private property and as a result had violated a city ordinance.

The police decided to give us both tickets for criminal trespassing. We had no idea that we were trespassing, but the police officers didn't want to hear it. We argued our positions as much as we could, but in the end they still gave us both a ticket.

My best friend didn't mind the ticket as much as I did. With my future in mind I couldn't afford to have a criminal record. I knew it would make my life a lot harder in a variety of ways. My father's dream was at stake and it couldn't end like this. I had to figure out a way to ensure that regardless of what happened, I wouldn't get a criminal record and ruin my future job prospects.

I took off time from school to go to Omaha for the initial hearing on the criminal trespassing charge. I wore a full suit, while my friend Brandon dressed in slacks and a casual button-down shirt with no tie. We walked into a crowded courtroom and sat in the back, patiently waiting for our names to be called. As I looked around the room, I noticed that a significant number of the people there had been at the night club the evening of the incident and must be in attendance for the same charge.

One by one I watched young Blacks get up from their seats when called upon and be read their rights by the judge. The judge would go on to give them the option of pleading guilty or not guilty. The judge would note that if found guilty, they could face the maximum amount of jail time for the criminal trespassing charge, which was a year. But if they immediately pled guilty, they would merely be slapped on the wrist and be required to pay a $50 fine.

It seemed like an obvious choice for every young person who walked in front of the judge. With consistency, they all chose the $50 fine. I thought to myself that along with the judge's disclaimer, he forgot to mention how a criminal record can instantly dissolve a bright future.

As we could sense that our time to be called upon was near, my best friend Brandon turned to me and whispered, "I think I'm going to plead guilty and just pay the fine." I replied, "Not me. Although I can't afford a lawyer, I can't afford a criminal record even more." He agreed. That day in court at least fifteen people were charged with criminal trespassing. Only two of them pleaded not guilty.

I called everyone I knew for a reference to a good lawyer. My best friend decided to take his chances with a public defender. I finally was referred to a young criminal defense attorney who had built an impressive track record. His going rate for my type of charge was $1,500 and I only had $700 left in my bank account. After a little coaxing he took my case for $700. I couldn't afford to hire a lawyer, but I wasn't going to put a price on my future.

While I waited to hear from my defense attorney, the costs I had paid for a lawyer immediately forced me to improvise my living situation. My mother brought me to a church that gave out free food every weekend. I grew up doing the same type of thing and I hated doing it at an older age. It reminded me of everything that I regretted about growing up poor, and it made me even more upset that I had gone back to that point. Regardless of how embarrassed I was, I needed the food and kindly accepted it anyway.

In the meantime, I put everything I had into studying hard and trying to ensure that I made the grades necessary to continue on to the next year. After a while my defense attorney contacted me and informed me that he had plea bargained with the prosecutor's office and was able to get the charges dropped in exchange for community service.

My best friend's public defender had failed to get him any type of deal. My lawyer contacted my friend's public defender and informed her of a plea deal that he had solidified on my behalf. We were both able to have the charges dropped in exchange for a few weeks of community service.

Once again it was an unfortunate fact that I couldn't go back to my old neighborhood to socialize, because of its reputation for violence. Maybe I had been wrong for being in that environment, but whether I was wrong or not, I learned to always be careful and to stay focused on my goals. With everything I was trying to accomplish, I knew how important keeping my nose clean was.

If I were to plead guilty to a criminal trespassing charge, my life would have been flipped upside down. Regardless of the unwanted legal drama, I wasn't going to let it distract me from the mission I had come so far to accomplish. I wondered if my father had dealt with similar situations on his journey toward the fulfillment of his dreams.

The end of my second semester rolled around and so did finals. Although I had studied harder than I ever had in my life, I was extremely nervous. Everything I had worked for was on the line, and I didn't have anything to fall back on. I thought about the embarrassment I would face and all the people I would let down if I flunked out of law school. I had a bachelor's degree in legal communications, but it was pretty useless and not much to fall back on if I didn't go to law school.

One of my Black law school friends had actually flunked out of his first year and after making an appeal to a committee of faculty, administration, and students had been allowed to repeat his first year. I remember asking him, "What was the process like just in case I am forced to take the same steps that you had taken?" He replied sternly, "Don't think like that because it's something to be avoided at all costs."

My finals week was full of rigorous studying, prayer, and caffeine pills. I knew my dad was somewhere watching all of this unfold. I only wished that he were close enough to give me the encouragement that I so desperately needed. It had been nineteen years since I had last seen my father, and not even the slightest dream had relieved me of my yearning to hear his voice again. It would be at this moment, with the mental fatigue and heavy burden of others' hopes clinging to my potential that I would need his guidance more than ever.

My mother told me once when I was younger that if I thought about my father before I went to sleep, I would see him in my dreams. Unfortunately, in my experience that had never worked. This time I wrote "Dad, I need you" on a piece of notebook paper and placed it under my pillow before my first final. That night I would see my father for the first time since his untimely passing.

> "If I thought about my father before I went to sleep, I would see him in my dreams."

The lights in my bedroom were dim as I sat in my bedroom closet with smeared tears on my face. The feeling of defeat had completely demoralized any motivation that had yet to seep from my soul. It wasn't long before I began to hear a voice outside my bedroom door. It was a voice whose sound time had yet to escape from my memory. It was the voice of my father.

I remember him talking to a third person whose identity I couldn't make out. My father expressed how proud of me he was. He went on to say, "Everything will work out." At that moment in my life he told me exactly what I needed to hear. That week I continued to study as hard as I physically and mentally could, and the rest I left up to fate.

My first year of law school I was hardly involved with any extracurricular activities. Most first years were too busy with their class schedule and assignments to think about anything else. During finals week I had been invited to a meeting for the Black Law Students Association. A meeting was being held because a new executive board would be voted upon for the next school year.

I had completely forgotten about the meeting and coincidently walked past the room where the meeting was being held. I was quickly ushered inside the room by a few of my classmates. During the meeting all of the executive positions had been taken, except the position of president. A few of my classmates nominated me for the position, but I honestly didn't want it.

I was still timid about the possibility of flunking out of school, and I didn't want any further embarrassment. I also was unsure whether or not I would be able to handle the responsibility of running the organization and simultaneously performing well in school. After an informal vote I was elected president, which gave me even more motivation to perform well on my final exams. I had to pass my classes so that I could return in the fall to head the organization.

Less than a month after finals my grades came back. The law school required that every student's grades be calculated after each year, and if your grades were anything less than a C average, you would be unable to continue. Our law school also had a unique grading scale that ranged from zero, being an F, to nine, which was an A+. A 4.0, which was a C average, was the lowest grade average that you could receive in order to advance to the next year.

I anxiously opened the envelope I had received in the mail containing my first year grades. I saw that I had one C+ which was a five, three C's which were all fours, and two D+'s which counted as threes. After adding the value of my first year grades I received, and then dividing by the number of classes I had taken, my grade average equaled a 4.0 exactly! I had just barely made it by the skin of my teeth. If one teacher had even given me a C instead of a C+ or a D+ instead of a C, I would have flunked out of law school entirely.

The news was sobering. My dream was still alive but that didn't change the fact that my grades needed to improve. Our first semester grades equaled a certain percentage of our overall first year grades, so I was sure that my first semester was a major factor in dragging down my grades. Either way I had made it to the second year and there was no point in stressing myself over the summer, so I decided not to think about it until school started again in the fall.

Although my grades had been too low to get any summer associate positions at any law firms, somehow I still found work. I ended up landing a job in Omaha teaching criminal law and justice to inner city high school students through the Urban League. The program was called Urban League University, and classes were conducted at a high school on the North side of town close to where I grew up. I had never taught a class before, but I had worked with inner city youth in the past and was sure I would be able to relate with them being that I had once been in their shoes.

The program didn't have the budget to provide the kids with books and there was no curriculum outlined for us, so I was forced to create an entire eight-week curriculum from scratch. I didn't know much about criminal justice, but I had just taken criminal law in the fall and still had my class materials from the course. I also had my laptop and thought the kids would be more engaged if I used PowerPoint presentations to accompany instruction.

I watered down the material but only slightly. I thought it would be beneficial for the kids to gain confidence by being able to comprehend professional course material. I also thought it was important to show the kids that you could pursue academics and still be cool. I was determined to take this job seriously not only because of my previous negative law firm experience, but because I wanted to positively impact the kids anyway I could as I saw a lot of me in them.

One of my students in particular reminded me exactly of how I was when I was a young and optimistic senior in high school. Reggie was tall for his age and often caught the attention of the younger girls in the classroom. I could see the same fire in his eyes that had taken me this far. Before he had any idea, I had made up my mind that I was going to mentor him.

Reggie had moved to Nebraska fresh from the deep South. Before moving from the South, he had regularly skipped school and had been failing the majority of his classes. His father, whom he now stayed with, sold drugs and had been in and out of jail. Neither of his parents had ever graduated from high school.

On a weekend while standing outside at my best friend Brandon's house, I heard someone call out, "Mr. Garrett!" I knew it could only be one of my students, and as I turned around I saw Reggie standing there in a T-shirt, basketball shorts, and sandals. He talked in depth about his living situation and how he was struggling to make ends meet, but that he wanted more. He wanted to go to college.

I knew exactly how he felt. He wanted to chase the same dream that I had pursued for so many years. But I had heard so many kids talk about hollow ambitions and dreams with no action ever taken toward making them real. I told him if he was serious to call me. I gave him my contact information and he contacted me consistently regarding college from that day on.

I talked to Reggie's mother often on the phone, helping them both walk through whatever stumbling blocks that they faced in the college application or financial aid process. I had a few contacts at the local community college that I put him in touch with. If there was anything that I could do to stop his similar recurring cycles, I was going to do everything within my power to help.

At night I worked at Home Depot as a seasonal sales associate in the garden and plumbing departments. When I started I didn't have any prior knowledge about plumbing or gardening, but regardless of the fact that it wasn't relevant to my career path, I still was intent on making a good impression. Overall, I was working seventy hours a week with both jobs combined.

I definitely was fatigued but ignored it because I needed the money. More than anything I needed to save up to buy a car. At the time, I was catching a ride to and from work with friends in exchange for gas money. Since my job was in Omaha and my apartment was in Lincoln, I was forced to stay with my best friend Brandon and his family again. His mother was kind enough to give me a key to the house and allow me to have the basement to myself. With both jobs keeping me busy, it wasn't hard for the summer to fly right by. I was still willing to do whatever it took to get where I wanted to be.

Before I knew it, both of my summer jobs had ended, and I was looking forward to returning to school. I had saved up enough money to buy a car. The car was pretty cheap and was all I could afford, but I was proud to have transportation again. My girlfriend had also graduated from Howard that spring and had moved to Lincoln to stay with me and work for a year. After such a lonely and depressing first year, I welcomed her company.

As my second year began, I worked harder than I did the first year. I was on academic probation because of my lackluster performance during my first year and knew that I still could flunk out of school if something didn't change. I also found it difficult to balance all of my obligations. My position as president of the Black Law Students

Association required so much of my time that I was scared it would affect my academic performance in school.

Looking back, my involvement in the organization was probably the best thing that happened to me during law school. I started to become more social, and law school overall became more enjoyable. I took the position seriously and hosted as many speakers and events as I could. I even had discovered that with a twist of irony, my father had been the co-founder of Creighton Law School's Black Law Students Association, which was the only other law school in the state.

The second year dragged by, but the first year gave me the confidence to get through it. I made sure I did everything that I didn't do during my first year and was determined to do well. I often heard that once you make it through your first year of law school the rest is a piece of cake. That proved to be far from true during my experience.

The classes were just as difficult as the first year. Our assignments were significantly longer and our teachers understandingly expected more. During my first year I was rarely vocal in class, which was not my personality at all, but this year I made a genuine effort to participate more. Between the Black Law Students Association and my rigorous schedule, I started to feel overwhelmed. Mentally I was tired, and I didn't know how much longer I could stay focused.

During the middle of the semester my car broke down. After taking it to have the problem diagnosed,

I was told that the engine was gone and the car was useless. I fell into a deeply depressed state after finding out that I would be forced to go without again. I had used the car to take my girlfriend to and from work, and my mom was depending on me to take her to get her prescription medication. Regardless, I couldn't afford to waste time dwelling on things I had no control of.

While I sat studying at the same dining room table that I felt I never left, I received a text message from my best friend Brandon. He told me that my old mentee Reggie had come by his house to tell me that he had gotten into college. Looking up and away from my phone, I smiled the most genuine smile that my face had seen in a long time. After dwelling on Reggie's accomplishment for a few moments, I put my head back down and continued to immerse myself in my study materials.

Finals rolled around once again and I engrossed myself in my studies. My girlfriend started to feel alienated and I felt bad because I was the only person that she really knew in the entire state. But she knew how important this was for me and gave me the space I needed to do well. When it came time to actually take my exams, I did what I always did, I prayed and I left it up to the powers that be.

During Christmas break, I flew to Detroit to spend Christmas with my mother and my sister. It was only the second time that I saw my sister since the accident. She had regained her ability to walk but still had nerve damage in her right leg and had not yet recovered fully.

She had applied to receive permanent disability and was awarded it. It was hard to comprehend that both my mother and sister were disabled. I felt guilty simply because I was healthy. I was determined to find a way to make things better for my family.

Things began to go against me when I discovered that my sister had resorted to drugs again. Before I had come to Detroit my mother had been visiting with my sister and one of her cousins, when he emerged from the kitchen with a plate of cocaine. He possibly may have been thinking that my mother was still on drugs.

While discussing my sister's drug habit, I asked my sister why she would do that to herself and her daughter, when she directly observed how much drugs had negatively affected our family. I knew she had been depressed because the accident had taken away much of her youth, but she had to be strong for her daughter. She had to be strong for us. She agreed that I was right, but I don't think my words changed her frame of mind. I yearned for a taste of a normal life, but then again what is normal?

When I returned to school, my grades came back from my previous semester. I did better than I had done the previous year, but it still was not enough to get me off academic probation. My spring semester would prove to be my most challenging yet.

Toward the beginning of the spring semester my relationship with my girlfriend wasn't doing well and we temporarily separated. Shortly thereafter, while at the dining room table trying to make the most out of my time studying, I learned one of my closest friends had drowned while swimming in Cancun. In an effort to cope with the death of my friend who had drowned, the night I found out, I used liquor to drown the pain. Both would take a huge toll on my motivation to study.

> "I yearned for a taste of a normal life, but then again what is normal?"

I also was in dire need of a vehicle, and after my last car's engine went out the semester before, I wasn't sure about getting another car. But I knew that I was going to need a car in order to be able to get to work during the upcoming summer. My cousin Brett, who was currently living in Georgia, had a 1994 Jeep Cherokee that I could use. Brett had also been present alongside Bianca when my father had passed. In an effort to take advantage of the opportunity, I flew down to Georgia to take a truck off his hands. He was getting ready to ship out to Afghanistan in what would be his third tour to Afghanistan to take part in the war effort.

As I drove back from Georgia, I drove through the worst snowstorm that the Southeast had seen in years. I could barely see a few car lengths in front of me as I maneuvered through a never-ending blanket of snow. Traveling through the blizzard with balding tires, I hit black ice a few times and the truck began to hydroplane. While my life flashed before my eyes, I thought about a dream that I had yet to complete. The things we do while chasing our ambitions can be insane.

As I drove by, I could see countless cars that had wrecked on the side of the road. I prayed that I would make it back home safe. Driving alone for hours gave me time to reflect. Heading down the Interstate all I could think about was finishing what I had begun.

Between the plane ticket to get down there, and gas during the fourteen-hour trip from south Georgia to Nebraska, I was on my last few nickels and dimes. But I was willing to make the sacrifice knowing that I needed transportation to get to wherever my internship would be during the upcoming summer. I had become accustomed to doing whatever I had to do.

When I finally got back to school, the Associate Dean called me into her office. In so many ways, she told me that I needed to get my act together or I wouldn't make it to the next year. I knew she was right, and I had to figure out what it was that was a barrier to improving my performance.

I knew that it was a real possibility that I could still flunk out of school if I didn't do better. I was frustrated. I hadn't been accustomed to being toward the bottom of the bell curve. Still, I couldn't quit. I had come way too far to turn back now.

I promised myself that I would do whatever it took to make it to the next year and also get off academic probation. I forced myself to spend more hours in the library and used whatever study aids I could get my hands on. I studied in groups as much as I could, so that I could gauge how well I was learning the class material in comparison to my peers. I also talked with my professors more often in order to find ways to learn the material more efficiently.

This time when finals came, I was ready. While taking each exam I felt more comfortable with the material and was even looking forward to showing my professors what knowledge I had retained. When my grades came back, I had scored in the top 20 percent in most of my classes and had finally performed well enough to get off academic probation. But more importantly, I had made it to the next year and my dream was still alive.

In law school there are two major ways to make your resume stand out: either get on law review or intern/clerk for a judge. Since I wasn't at the top of my class and I didn't make law review, I badly needed something else to help my resume stand out. Mentoring would come through for me once again.

Gail was tall and thin and everything about her screamed high society. She carried herself well and was youthful in her outlook on life. Until recently, Gail had been the Executive Director of MENTOR. I had known her for years and she had taken an active role in mentoring me.

Her daughter-in-law was a district court judge in South Florida and had offered me the opportunity to

- intern with her. The major issues for me would be how I would get to Fort Lauderdale, and since it was an unpaid internship, how would I be able to afford to do it. After careful consideration, the only option was for me to take summer courses and use whatever financial aid I was refunded in order to pay for living expenses.

I wanted to keep my apartment in Lincoln because of its close proximity to the law school but, unfortunately, due to my leasing agreement I couldn't sublease it. As a result, I would have to pay for rent there and in Florida. Florida compared to Lincoln was an insanely expensive place to live even if only for two months. After calculating the money that I would have from my financial aid refund check and my overall expenses, I would have just enough money to pay for everything. It seemed as if I always found a way to fuel my dreams.

10

THE APPIAN WAY

In the midst of battle in my right hand I wielded resilience,
while in my left I held my father's torch burning brilliant.

While an empire had failed to heed ancient lessons, we
headed down paved streets as byproducts of oppression.

In large droves we were joined by the maimed and the old,
taking time to pay reverence to the motionless who lined
the road.

Along the way to conquer the city of dreams, I was willing
to spread my arms and sacrifice everything.

In early June, my girlfriend and I packed up our belongings and got ready to hit the road. She had been accepted into a graduate program on the East Coast, and I was dropping her off back at home in Atlanta for the summer on the way to Florida. After careful deliberation we decided that the best way to get there would be to drive. I knew it would put a lot of miles on my truck, and as a result I did everything from buying new tires to a full diagnostic and oil change. I figured if I could make the trip from Georgia, than I could make the trip to Florida.

When we were finally on the road everything seemed to be going well. The truck was packed full of our belongings from front to back, and we were both excited to be starting a new stage in our lives. We were only a half hour outside Nebraska when things started to go wrong.

The car had begun to make strange noises, and I could see from the temperature gauge that it was overheating. As the engine started smoking, I pulled off to the side of the road. With the amount of smoke coming from the engine, I knew it couldn't be good. This was just my luck; we hadn't even been on the road an hour.

As we looked around we were in the middle of nowhere. Luckily we weren't too far from an onramp that led to a small town in Missouri. We both grabbed a couple of our belongings and walked about a mile before we found a truck stop with a small service station. We walked inside and asked whether they would be able to service the truck. After they suggested that we bring the truck in so they could have a look, we had the truck towed there in hopes that they could service it.

As we waited for what seemed like an eternity, the weather started to get bad. The wind started to pick up, and we could see menacing clouds hanging overhead. Before we knew it, rain was pouring down, and the wind was howling. Most of the semi-trucks had pulled out of the station in an effort to beat the storm. Eventually, everyone at the truck stop had ceased what they were doing and stood outside looking up at the dark sky. Slowly the clouds overhead started to rotate, and we decided that it would be in our best interest to go inside.

The inside of the truck stop didn't seem to be any safer, with hundreds of jagged metal truck parts and accessories dangling and clinking all around us. We went inside a small waiting room to see what the news was saying about the weather. They had just issued a tornado warning for the county we were in. Just when we thought things couldn't get any worse, the car repair man told us that they didn't have the equipment necessary to service the truck.

It was almost ten o'clock at night, and there wasn't anything else that we could do at that point until the morning. We decided to brave the wind and rain and headed for a motel across the street to spend the night. The room smelled of smoke. It lacked all the amenities that you would normally find in even the lowest budget motels.

As I lay down in bed that night to go to sleep, a thousand thoughts raced through my mind. More than anything, I was sorry that my girlfriend had to be there to go through the inconvenient ordeal. Regardless, the opportunity in Florida was too great to pass up. Before I closed my eyes I decided that I would get there no matter what it took.

The next day we checked out of the motel early and walked over to the service station to weigh our options. The closest full service station was in St. Joseph, Missouri, which was about seventy miles south of us. It was our best chance to fix the truck and get back on the road. With only a thousand dollars to get me through the summer, I had already spent an alarming amount on the vehicle at this point.

Towing the truck to St. Joseph cost me another significant portion of my savings. My money was running low, but I was sure things would somehow make a turn for the better. We finally arrived in St. Joseph and grabbed some lunch while the truck was looked at. After about an hour I finally got a phone call from the service station and the news was grim.

The truck's engine had gone out, and what it would cost to repair it was more than the car was worth. My Aunt Mary Ann lived about another seventy miles south of our current location in St. Joseph in Kansas City. With the truck belonging to her son Brett, she advised me to get it towed down to her house, and we would figure out the rest when we got there. I couldn't afford to get it towed again and just wanted to get a rental car in St. Joseph and then drive the rest of the way.

Still, I just couldn't abandon my cousin's car so we decided to have it towed to Kansas City anyway. After an hour drive, seventy miles, and another cut into my dwindling savings, the tow truck unhitched the Jeep. I was soon pushing the heavy truck into my aunt's driveway up a steep incline by myself.

At that point we could either rent a car and drive the rest of the way or buy a plane ticket and ship the rest of our belongings. We carefully weighed our options and decided that renting a car would be the cheapest way to get there. The only problem was that neither I nor my girlfriend was old enough to rent a car, and we didn't own a credit card required to secure one. There were a few places that accepted debit cards, but none of them would give us a one-way rental. No one that we knew had a credit card either, no one except my mother, and she was three hours away back in Lincoln.

Right when we were ready to drive my aunt's car back to Lincoln and start all over, my girlfriend found a cheap rental rate on the Internet. A friend of the family who was over twenty-five was also willing to rent the car for us. Finally, we were on the road and headed to Atlanta.

The drive was about fourteen hours and I drove most of the way. We arrived in Atlanta late on a Thursday night. My girlfriend's parents were going through an awkward divorce. Between her parents and three younger siblings there wasn't any room for us at her parents, so we stayed with one of her close friends. Over the next three days I tried to forget about everything that had happened to me, but in the back of my mind I couldn't help thinking about how I would survive over the summer with what little money I had left.

Saturday night came and I kissed my girlfriend goodbye and got back on the road alone. The drive from Atlanta to Fort Lauderdale was about ten hours. I had scheduled to meet the landlord for the property I was renting early in the morning. I made the majority of the drive at night. As the sun began to light up the eastern sky, I was within Fort Lauderdale city limits.

I left the freeway and turned onto the city's unclean streets for the first time. When I was stopped at a street light, I looked on either side of me, and it didn't take long to notice that I was in the heart of the Haitian ghetto. It reminded me of home. Seeing Hispanics, Blacks, the disabled, and the old, I was immediately reminded of the story of Spartacus, when his thirst for change took him down the Appian Way toward the gates of Rome, and he witnessed a road lined with his fellow forgotten peers.

When I finally pulled up to my destination, the landlord arrived about a half hour later. The property was a duplex with each separate residence containing a studio-style apartment. Each side of the duplex was available so the landlord gave me a tour of both. The outside of the property was pretty poorly kept, but the inside of the first duplex seemed rather decent. Just when I had about made up my mind to live in the first duplex, we walked into the bedroom where a large insect was lying dead in the middle of the floor. What had I gotten myself into I wondered?

As we walked into the second duplex it was rather inviting and from what I could see the conditions were suitable. I paid the landlord for the two months' rent and remembered that the rental car was due within the next two hours. I hurried up and went to the closest Walmart that I could find to buy groceries. After paying for the rental car and gas, I only had about a hundred dollars to my name left over from my depleted savings.

I didn't have much time to shop for groceries methodically, so I just grabbed whatever I could. I tried my best to keep a tally in my head of how much everything was. When I arrived at the cash register, I was just within a few dollars of what I could afford to purchase, while still having money to fill the rental with gas. I hurried back to the house to unload the few groceries that I had bought and raced toward the airport to drop the rental car off.

I filled the gas tank at a filling station within five minutes of the airport and arrived about fifteen minutes before the car was due. I knew the car wasn't in my name, so I wanted to make the dropoff as quick and problem free as I could. As I gave the agent my rental documents, the price for the rental came to over $600, which for some reason was much more than our family friend had originally been quoted. As a result the credit card was rejected.

I told the agent that couldn't be the right price, because with the deal that we had been quoted it was only supposed to be $150. With very little empathy the agent told me to take it up with the cashier at the front desk. Well there were two problems with this.

First, I wasn't supposed to be driving the car in the first place, so if they discovered that I wasn't the rightful driver, they would charge our family friend's card even more. Second, I didn't have $600 to pay them and had no desire to find out what would happen once they found out that I couldn't pay. I thought the best thing to do would be to have our family friend resolve the issue over the phone.

Instead of walking toward the cashier to pay, I walked right past him. As soon as I was inside the airline terminal, I tried to get as far away as I could. I called my best friend Brandon, who was in town for the weekend, to come and pick me up. While waiting for him to get there, I pulled my hat down over my face and hood over my head, anticipating my name and description to be called on the terminal loudspeaker at any moment. When my best friend finally arrived, I quickly walked outside and hopped inside the car and told him to quickly drive off.

I couldn't believe everything that I had been through in the last few days. All I wanted to do was take advantage of a great opportunity and get one step closer to fulfilling my dream. In an odd twist of irony my father had also worked for a judge in Florida during his law school career. I could only imagine what he had sacrificed to get there.

With hardly any money in my pockets, I had no idea how I would even get back home to Nebraska at the end of the summer. I knew I needed to make temporary sacrifices for long-term gains, but I was hardly prepared for what those sacrifices would be. But I had been on the ropes countless times before, and I refused to lie down for the count.

The judicial internship was going great, and I was getting a lot of practical experience. I was working for the district court judge in the family division. My judge was really good at explaining everything to me and often included me in her thought process while making judgments. I was extremely fond of her and did my best to do well at every task I was given.

Every time I was free I sat in on trials in other courtrooms watching lawyers and trying to suck up all the knowledge I could. I was nervous. I just wanted to do well. I had learned a lot from my previous experience at the law firm and was determined not to let Gail down like I had let down James.

While I sat in on criminal trials, every single person that I saw sentenced to a prison term shared my African heritage. By the end of the summer I would see a drove of young Black males sent to prison. I personally knew what it was like to sit behind iron bars and they had my empathy. From personal experience, I knew how easy it was for a misguided Black youth to slightly veer from the right path and forever ruin his life. It was at that point that I questioned my promotion of a flawed legal system that was sending my own people to prison in disproportionate numbers.

After I left work I didn't have much of a social life. Overall, I didn't know anyone in Fort Lauderdale and took the social seclusion pretty hard. I didn't have any money to even go anywhere so that I could meet people, and even if I did, I lacked the transportation to get there. At night I came home to an empty house. My confinement began to breed depression. I barely had enough money to ride on the bus to and from work. I wanted to give up and began to wonder why I had even left the comfort of Nebraska in the first place.

> " It was a congregation of the forgotten."

On a Wednesday things really started to get to me. I had eight bucks to my name and not the slightest idea when I would get any again. The fact that two men become involved in a violent dispute immediately next to me as I waited for the bus didn't help my mood any either. I looked around the downtown Fort Lauderdale bus terminal, where the air was filled with unpleasant odors, and people traversed to and fro with soiled clothing and pessimistic expressions. It was a congregation of the forgotten.

During the bus ride home I kept to myself immersed in my thoughts. I felt that I had done everything that anybody could ask a kid to do. I could feel myself getting to the point of not caring anymore. Just when emotionally I felt I had reached my breaking point, something changed my outlook.

I had been closely watching a young Black woman with wild and untidy hair. Her glasses were obviously broken and as crooked as any I had ever seen. In the hands of each of her three children, I saw a box of cereal. They were all happier than I had seen anyone in a long time. I looked around and saw all of the other passengers' faces light up while watching how happy the children were. I envied the innocence of their youth, which had yet to be corrupted by the cares of the world.

They didn't care if their hair was neat, or the fact they were forced to carry groceries while riding the bus. They saw the good in their situation despite what everyone else on that bus may have seen. At that moment I saw the good in my own situation and reminded myself about my promise never to give up.

During the next few weeks things started to get somewhat better. Gail and James came into town on separate occasions. It was a relief to see familiar faces and for a second I was able to forget about all of my worries. My girlfriend even came down to visit for a weekend. I felt bad that I didn't have the money to take her out or show her around. Still, we made the best of it.

When it was time for each of them to go, I felt as if they were sailing away and leaving me on a deserted island. I was tired of being alone. In their absence I was able to get together with a college friend who was a prosecutor in Miami. It was nice to visit him in Miami, but I couldn't really enjoy being there with so few dollars in my pocket and so many worries on my mind.

My internship continued to go well. With each project I was given, I performed to the best of my ability and continually received more challenging projects. When I had been working at my previous internship at the Washington, D.C., law firm, I remembered complaining to James how I was never given stimulating tasks to complete. He told me that I needed to be able to excel at the work that I was already given, and if I did well I would be given more difficult tasks. He was right, and I had taken his advice to heart and was going to give 200 percent toward even the most menial tasks.

As my internship came to a close, money was nonexistent. I had about a dollar and some change in my bank account and a few dollars in cash on me. I had to make sure I ate breakfast before I went to work because I didn't have money for lunch. After two months of not eating right, I started to lose weight. This was the blessing that I had asked for and I was going to see it through.

That summer I didn't have to work at my internship every day, but I was there every day faithfully in an attempt to gain as much practical experience as I possibly could. But with no money during the last two weeks, I could only afford to go to work once or twice a week. I also was taking nine summer law school credits, so I told my judge that I was taking time out to get caught up in my school work. I had surpassed the hours she initially had expected me to work so she didn't mind. I didn't want her to know that I couldn't afford to catch the bus to work every day.

That summer I had a lot of time to myself to think. I had a chance to evaluate my future and to reevaluate my past. I still wanted to fulfill my father's dream more than ever and to help my own people. Yet, I was tired of financial instability and struggling in so many aspects of life. I was determined when I went back to school that I was going to work harder than ever. In the midst of not having any finances, my girlfriend scrambled up some money and bought me a cheap plane ticket back home. Now that I had a way back home, I had to figure out how to get my belongings there too. Since I had a plane ticket I would have to ship them. But how?

I had less than a week left in Fort Lauderdale before I was scheduled to fly home. My Aunt Mary Ann informed me that a distant cousin was going to be in Fort Lauderdale and wanted to link up with me. Luckily for me, her husband just so happened to work for FedEx, and she was able to ship my belongings back home. It never ceases to amaze me how something always develops out of nothing.

Before my cousin left town, she offered me a roll of cash. I kindly rejected her offer when she retorted, "Aunt

Mary Ann said you don't have anything to eat." This
was untrue. I had just enough food to last me until my
internship was over and it was time for me to go back
home. I admit there were times when I wasn't eating
right over the summer but it didn't worry me because I
had experienced worse.

Throughout my process of sacrifice and maturation
I didn't want pity. All that I desired was support more
so mental and emotional as opposed to monetary. This
had been the first summer since I turned fourteen that
I hadn't worked for profit. I had come down to South
Florida for no pay with the purpose of proactively turning
my ambitions into something tangible. I wasn't looking
for a handout, I was just trying to find my own way.

Every day my experiences were teaching me that
if you want something and are willing to go through
hell to get it, then it's yours. When my car broke down
at the beginning of the summer, I had no idea how I
was going to get to Florida. When I finally got down
to Florida, I had no idea how I was going to make it
through the summer or most importantly how I would
get back home.

Somehow a way had been made and I was excited to get
back home to finish my last year of law school. I had come
far but I hadn't reached my dreams just yet. I had to cross
that stage at graduation first, and it wouldn't be the end but
only the beginning. My degree would take me down a long
hallway of open doors and I knew that through each door
lay unlimited potential to find greatness.

Sometimes I would close my eyes and imagine what it would feel like not to have to worry about money. If I wanted to take a vacation within the next six months, I wanted to be able to do it. I wanted to be able to help my family and one day have the monetary resources to support a family of my own. I didn't have any natural talents. I put my faith in my drive and ambition.

I had bitten the fruit of knowledge and knew that there was so much more to life than the things I had already experienced. I wanted badly to see the world and to make a difference in it. But like I had always told myself, before I could help anyone else I was going to have to first help myself. I had proudly followed my father's footsteps farther than I ever thought I would, but I had so much farther to go.

> "Faith is not knowing how far the finish line is, but believing that one day you'll get there."

It was the last day of my internship and my judge gave me a ride home. She was sad to see me go, and I was appreciative of the opportunity I had been given. Over the summer we had built a meaningful relationship and she had been a friendly face during my time there. There were numerous times when I had thought I wasn't strong enough to make it to the end. But faith is not knowing how far the finish line is, but believing that one day you'll get there. If my father could see me, I just hoped he was proud of my sacrifice for our dream.

When I finally arrived home in Omaha, I stayed at my best friend Brandon's house as always. I would have preferred to stay at my own house in Lincoln, but I didn't have any money to buy groceries for my apartment. My mother's house in Lincoln was also too small to accommodate me. I knew that everything I was sacrificing would one day pay off.

I had some remaining school work that took up a lot of my time. For the most part while I was in Omaha I was just trying to stay out of trouble. I didn't want anything to happen that could jeopardize my scheduled graduation.

After a week or so of being home, another one of my best friends had informed me that he and a girl he was dating were going to have a baby. He would be the first out of my closest friends to do so and I was taken aback by the news. The baby had been a mistake and neither he nor the mother had the financial or educational base to provide for a child by themselves. Many of the people that I had grown up with had children at an early age. I always knew that with the things that I was trying to do, I couldn't bring a child into this world anytime soon. I barely could take care of myself and knew that a child would put many of my dreams on hold.

Because I grew up without a father, I knew I wanted to be there for my child and to make sure that my children were born into a household with married parents. I refused for my children to grow up fitting into

Black stereotypes and starting off as statistics waiting to happen. If I was going to ensure that my children didn't see any of the hard times I had endured, then not having children prematurely and out of wedlock was on the top of the to do list.

On one of the few nights that I went out, I ran into an old high school friend. He had played on my high school basketball team and had actually been pretty good. Since high school he had gone to college, but got caught up in selling crack. When things were good he could make over a thousand dollars in a single day. He also relished in the respect that he got from peers in his old neighborhood who saw selling drugs as admirable and even more impressive because he was also in college.

As his greed overcame him, he sold drugs to an undercover agent and in a split second his life was ruined. With gun and drug charges there wasn't much of a second chance for him. He praised Brandon and me for having degrees and told us that he wanted to follow our path. He knew that he had chased the wrong things: fast money, nice cars, and women. He had realized the folly of his ways but at this point it was too late.

On my way home that night I thought about everything we discussed. Growing up as a Black male it was so easy to throw your life away before you even realized what you were doing. My friend's situation could have easily been my own. I wanted to be part of the solution; I just didn't know what to do in order to be a catalyst for real change.

About a week later I had a conversation with another young Black male who was in his late twenties. He had just gotten out of prison from doing an eight-year term, and we never discussed what he had been convicted of. We had come from the same neighborhood but he had taken an entirely different path. He was a prime example of a troubled Black male who had no direction, and his path toward destruction was seemingly unstoppable.

I wish that I could have talked to him before he threw his life away. I wanted to reach out to other Black males who, like me, wanted a way out but hadn't had the luck that I had. A couple of my friends who were present during the conversation conveyed that many of my peers looked up to me for being an example of how to make it out of the ghetto. My way was the long way and few had the patience or endurance to take such a route. Hearing that made me determined to finish law school and ever more determined to make sure that I shared my story.

It was the weekend before law school started and it was time to head back to school. Brandon's brother had moved back in the house along with his twin sisters that were already staying there, so space was extremely limited. With less than five dollars to my name, my rent was late and my phone was getting ready to get cut off. Like every semester right before school starts, I was waiting on my refund check so that I could get my life in order.

Before I was any more of a burden to Brandon and his family, I decided that it was time to head back to Lincoln. I hoped that my days of instability and having to rely on so many other people would soon come to an end.

I had finally arrived back in Lincoln and things started out pretty rough. Without much money between my roommate and me, the first month back at school proved to be challenging. My mother helped us out by bringing us food from the church mission where she volunteered. Growing up, I had many bad experiences with donated food and would only turn to it in dire circumstances. Financial aid from my school arrived later than usual that year. In the meantime I just had to make things work.

During the beginning of the school year I was mentally, emotionally, and academically drained. At the start of the semester, I had turned in two thirty-page papers for my summer courses on complex issues, which took a lot out of me. When classes began, I dragged my feet and wasn't completely engaged in my schoolwork. Everyone has slumps when you feel like life is getting the best of you. The key is to make sure that you never stay in a slump for long. I had struggled all my life, so what was one more year?

As the semester progressed, my mind had failed to find peace. I constantly tossed and turned in my sleep. When asked by family members whether I was eating right, I lied. Almost midway through the last lap toward bringing substance to my dreams, my lungs were gasping for air. The gravity of having to walk a thousand miles while carrying the hopes of those dear to me was unnerving, but if I not me then who? The burden of my family's hopes and dreams had been carried by my father before me, and now it was mine to bear. Although weary, rest was a luxury I couldn't afford.

When finals came I tried my best to push through it. Almost a week had gone by before I had gotten more than eight hours of sleep. Books and notebook paper were scattered throughout my apartment. During the times that I felt like lying down, I stood up. When I wanted to close my book and turn off the lights, I remembered when I didn't have any lights. On late nights when legal concepts had seemingly filled my mind until it was full, I reminded myself of when my stomach had been empty.

> "When I wanted to close my book
> and turn off the lights, I remembered
> when I didn't have any lights."

All my life I had run away from poverty, but I still had not yet run far enough. To think that my success solely encompassed me would have been naïve. With all that in mind, I was dogged to finish what my father had started.

During my time at Howard, studying abroad had always been a consideration of mine. Unfortunately, I had never taken advantage of the opportunity during my undergraduate career. Because this would be my last year of law school, I was determined to step outside of my comfort zone and see the world before my academic career concluded.

I applied to and was accepted to participate in a study abroad program in the Middle East over my winter break. In an effort to pay the $2,400 tuition, I had meticulously saved money during the course of the previous semester. The only problem would be how I would afford to get there with plane ticket prices in the triple digits. After further monetary assistance from my mentor James, I finally had enough to pay everything.

The day after Christmas, and after a turbulence-filled fourteen-hour flight, I finally landed in Dubai. I had come to participate in a law and business program in an effort to see the world and maximize my professional growth. I grabbed my luggage from the baggage claim and converted a few American dollars into Emirate Dirhams, then headed outside into the unknown.

As I stepped into the cool desert air, I noticed that it was still dark outside, and suddenly I got cold feet. I had never been overseas before. I wondered what feelings overcame my father when he had journeyed to England during law school, similarly seeking to discover the world around him and his place in it.

I gathered my courage along with my luggage and finally hailed a cab. As we drove through downtown Dubai, I looked out the window and saw an endless sea of skyscrapers and neon lights. It was amazing that a little more than half a century ago Dubai had been nothing but sand for as far as the eye could see.

What seemed to me to be even more amazing was that I was a twenty-four-year-old Black male from the ghettos of Nebraska that somehow came to be in the Middle East. I thought that if human ingenuity could take glass and metal and build a modern oasis from the desert sand, then with that same ingenuity I too could do anything.

The cab finally arrived where I would be staying for the remainder of the program: the Emirates Academy of Hospitality Management. The academy was known for producing premier students who would go straight into management positions, in many of the city's luxury hotels and resorts. After checking in at the security gate I headed to my room.

When I opened my room door and laid my bags down, fatigued from jet lag and the nine-hour time difference, I collapsed on what would be my bed for the next two weeks. But for some reason, regardless of how tired I was, I still couldn't sleep. I decided to step outside for a moment and get some fresh air.

The academy was directly across the street from the Burj al Arab, notoriously known as the world's only seven-star hotel. Shaped in the form of a sail blowing in the wind, the hotel had become the face and brand of Dubai. As I looked up at such an architectural feat, I remembered what I had come all this way for and promised myself that I would stay focused and make the absolute most of it.

The next morning, I woke up early and had hardly gotten any sleep the night before. I put on my most conservative casual attire and headed to the first day of class. The initial introduction to the program was held at the academy. The campus was pristine, equipped with an outdoor swimming pool, tennis courts, and amenities equal to that of some of the finest hotels in America.

As I walked into a modern classroom, I discovered that the vast majority of my fellow participants had already arrived. I looked around the room and saw the single most diverse group of individuals I had ever witnessed.

Most of the other students were from Germany, but others were from Cameroon, Australia, Morocco, Japan, the Netherlands, Bolivia, Malaysia, and a few others were also from America. I introduced myself to a German next to me and noticed a peculiar gold ring on his finger with strange symbols. When I asked him about the ring, he explained that it was his family shield—a family that traced its lineage back a thousand years.

I looked around the room and saw Rolexes on every other wrist and immediately understood the demographics of the group. I wasn't going to let any of that intimidate me. For most of them this was a casual vacation, but for me it was all business.

Although our introduction had been held at the academy all of our other lectures were held at the Dubai Women's College. The campus was located on the outskirts of Dubai and was one of the most beautiful campuses I had ever seen. Native Emirati women could be seen scurrying back and forth to class wearing burqas and other traditional Muslim attire. The college was one example of Sheik Mohammad Maktoum, the ruler of Dubai, making efforts to bring higher education to his people. Education was provided for free to the local Emirati women.

The two-week program was rigorous from the start. We received comprehensive lectures on everything ranging from Islamic banking law to hotel benchmarking. The program even included an introductory Arabic course. From 9 a.m. to 6 p.m. six days a week, we were occupied with courses and site visits. The site visits ranged from law firms and aluminum smelting plants, to FedEx's central Middle East logistics center.

Other site visits included tours to Dubai's free zones, which were areas meant to attract foreign investment. They served as conductors for the transportation of information and resources for international companies looking to do business in the Middle East or nearby emerging markets.

Whether I was sitting in class listening to a lecture, or visiting Dubai's International Financial Center, I was wholly engaged. From the day the program began, I made it a point to chase every networking opportunity that I saw. After every lecture, I made sure to catch the instructor and exchange business cards. During every site visit, I would sneak away from a lecture or tour in order to find lingering executives, ready with my contact information in hand. And at the end of the day I would send an email correspondence to the addresses of every business card that I had received.

After an event-filled day, while sitting in a dorm room into the early morning hours, we were well aware that we would dearly pay for it when we would have to wake up in a few hours. In the middle of a deep conversation I scanned the room. Together with me in the room sat two Germans, one Bolivian, and a native Emirate national. Representative of the first truly global generation, while we conversed, one thing was on all of our minds. We all felt that the old world order was crumbling. It was the same order that my own people across the African Diaspora and throughout the Third World had for centuries been victims of. It was the same order that was now failing the sick, old, and unemployed back in America. We all lived in a very different world than our parents had grown up in.

Although we lived on different continents throughout the world, the current international economic crisis that had engulfed the globe was ubiquitous. We all thirsted for change. It was amazing even with all of our economic or ethnic differences that as a new generation we were all on one accord.

Only a few days later, I sat uncomfortably in the back seat of a Nissan Maxima with a few other male participants from Morehouse College, which is another prestigious historically Black college located in

Atlanta, Georgia. In the driver and passenger seat sat two gorgeous native Emirati women. We were driving back from a joint outing with our program, along with students from the Dubai Women's College.

We all curiously shot questions back and forth about each other's religious beliefs and different cultures. Their country with all its riches also possessed hidden signs of the forgotten. The women told us stories of workers from India who were imported to work on building Dubai's vastly expanding infrastructure jumping in front of oncoming traffic committing suicide. Native Emiratis were forced to pay the victim's family the equivalent of $25,000 American dollars in compensation. The repulsive valuation of the worker's life was worth more than most of the workers would ever make in a lifetime.

We continued to exchange further questions. We discovered we were more alike than different. As Muslim women riding in the car with non-familial men, they were risking the consequences of harsh punishment. It seemed as optimistic young people, the ability to change existing paradigms lay within us. It was a life-changing experience and gave me the renewed hope and faith regarding the plight of the forgotten back home in America.

It wasn't long before the program was halfway over and New Year's Eve was upon us. To celebrate the evening's festivities, I chose to tag along with a few other participants who were bringing in the New Year by watching a fireworks show at the Burj Khalifa. The Burj Khalifa, at a height of half a mile, was the world's tallest man-made structure and a marvel of modern engineering. When midnight had finally arrived, the fireworks show began and fiery hues of every color could be seen shooting out of the Burj Khalifa itself, along with the surrounding skyscrapers.

As I looked up and watched the spectacular display of explosions illuminating the midnight sky, and in the midst of a new year, I reminisced about how far I had come and where I'd been. It was difficult to enjoy the moment, knowing that so many whom I had known would never get the chance to see such a vivid portrait. On my journey toward success I was ready to carry as many on my back as I conceivably could.

Days later during a day trip to the United Arab Emirate's capital, Abu Dhabi, I ate breakfast with both sleeves rolled up at a table made of palm wood. My dark shades blocked the penetrating glare of the early midday sun. My feet were cooled under the shade of the table while resting on top of the pristine white sand below me. I looked out into the ocean water as sunlight flickered off its rolling surface in a kaleidoscope of color. I wished I could take such a picturesque sight back home to those who remained in the ghetto.

Before I knew it the program had come to an end. During the parting banquet I said goodbye to friends whom I had made and was sure I'd have lasting relationships with. I had enjoyed my time there and was even more motivated than ever to realize my dream. I felt blessed to have been given the opportunity.

With fellow CBL International colleague Katsuhiko Furuhata (right), the author tours the sahan (courtyard) of the Sheik Zayed Grand Mosque in Abu Dhabi, U.A.E.

As soon as I returned home it was time to return to school for my last semester of law school. The trip to Dubai had left me fatigued. Two of my courses had already assigned a substantial amount of work while I had been overseas, and I hadn't been able to buy the textbooks until I had returned to the States. I began the semester extremely far behind. For the first week of class I found myself in a slump and unmotivated to do my work.

On top of my school work I also had other pressing thoughts on my mind. My sister had fallen into a deep depression and I was worried about her. She would express to me how unhappy she was with her unfortunate fate following her car accident. In the prime of her life, her youth and vigor had been snatched away. She couldn't drive anymore or finish school as she had intended. She was forced to walk with a cane and still faced painful rehabilitative therapy. Her doctors predicted that she would never return to her prior physical condition. Regardless of how much encouragement I gave her, I knew that coming from me, a young adult with no physical impairments, my words were hollow.

Around the same time, I had an in-depth conversation with my mother. She expressed how proud of me she was regarding how much I had achieved. She would say something that I would never forget. She told me, "Through your success and all of the things that you have had the opportunity to accomplish, I feel like I personally made it." Although she had failed to reach her own dreams, seeing her only son succeed provided her with a sense of achievement. She reminded me that I had made it so far because of my strength to endure, a strength that was far from common. Her words struck a deep chord and gave me the rejuvenation that I needed to keep going, while remembering those that were depending on me.

Less than a week after I had returned from Dubai I was scheduled to speak at the first annual National Mentoring Summit in Washington, D.C. I saw it as an opportunity to vent and speak my mind on issues that had been burdening my thoughts. Still drained from a busy schedule over the past month, I contemplated passing up the offer to speak at the event. The summit would be a two-day event held at the Library of Congress, and I would miss a significant amount of class by attending. But because of the magnitude of the event, it was an opportunity that would have been unwise to pass up.

On a Monday I arrived back in Washington, D.C. The evening before I was scheduled to speak at the summit, there was a VIP Reception for Board Members of MENTOR and its corporate partners, also held at the Library of Congress. After checking into my hotel I barely had a few hours to spare. I grabbed a bite to eat and tried in vain to get some homework done. Knowing that I didn't have the concentration to do any work I laid down hoping to get a half hour of sleep. It seemed like I had hardly laid my head on my pillow before the alarm clock jolted me awake.

I quickly put on a new suit I had recently bought and hailed a cab to the reception. When I arrived I discovered that it was a congregation of who's who in the nonprofit community. There were also a lot of prominent corporations present who were represented by various individuals. The board members of MENTOR were mostly the Wall Street types, but in an effort to expand the ideology of mentoring, they had made a lot of supportive connections spanning corporate America and the nonprofit community.

After networking, exchanging business cards, and drinking a few glasses of wine, I was called into a back room by the coordinator of the summit. I walked into a small room with a long wooden table covered with boxes, papers, and other supplies while aged books covered with dust lined the walls. At the end of the table sat a middle-aged white woman and an older gentlemen, neither whom I knew. I was introduced to both of them and discovered that the woman was the speech writer for the event, and the gentleman across from her was a board member. From his accent I guessed he was of Eastern European descent.

After introducing myself, he stared at me for a moment as if I were a child of his that he had not seen for decades. He formally introduced himself as Willem Kooyker, who was currently the Director of Fulton Financial, a multi-bank financial holding company that ranked among the Forbes Global 2000. He told me that he had funded and created the mentoring program that initially had been so instrumental to my success.

I quickly had a flashback to when I first walked into that room and saw Maggie sitting on the other side of the table. More than anything, I was surprised that out of all the engagements that I had spoken at on behalf of the organization that we had never met. I took the chance to sincerely thank him for all he had done, because without the opportunities that mentoring had provided me, I knew that things could have been a lot different.

Soon dinner had begun and I was sitting at a table next to the podium filled with high-powered players. To my immediate left sat Alan Schwartz, the former CEO of Bear Stearns, which had been the first bank bailed out during the commencement of the financial crisis by the Federal Reserve, and JPMorgan Chase where MENTOR co-founder Geoffrey T. Boisi had once been chairman. To my right sat Robert Woody, founder of Northstar Financial Services. Across the table sat Whitney R. Delich, the Senior Vice President of Human Resources at Viacom, who had made quite a name for herself after purchasing a Manhattan condo formerly belonging to the Clintons. Regardless of the economic disparity between myself and those around me, I felt at ease.

After dinner had been served and the last speaker had left the podium, Tonya wanted to show me something. Tonya was the Senior Vice President for MENTOR and had accompanied me previously when we had attended the taping of the *Oprah* show, including the following reception where I had met actor Hill Harper. I had gained an immense amount of respect for her, and she continued to be extremely supportive of everything I did.

She led me up a marble staircase leading to the third floor of the library. As soon as we arrived at the top of the staircase, waiting for me was a spectacular view. Where we were standing overlooked the main reading room of the library. It was a large circular room with a dome at the top of a high ceiling and was covered with breath-taking artwork. In the center of the room, a tall wooden podium rose from the floor like a large monolith protruding from the earth. She told me that this was where I would be delivering my speech the next morning. It would be by far the most impressive venue that I had the opportunity to speak, and I knew that I had to do well.

That night when I returned to my hotel room, I cancelled plans that I had made with some old friends from college. I felt ill prepared for the magnitude of tomorrow's occasion. I wanted more than ever to lie down and get some rest. Instead, I shrugged off my fatigue and pulled out my speech. I stayed up all night and painstakingly went over every word. I rehearsed the speech over and over until I looked at the time, and it was already half past five in the morning.

After getting less than two hours of sleep, I woke up and went over my speech a few more times. I put on my best suit, hailed a cab, and headed to the Library of Congress. I arrived at the event around 8:15 a.m., and grabbed a few cups of coffee, hoping that the caffeine would be able to give me enough energy to make it through the event. I walked into the reading room and found a seat away from everyone else. I continued to go over my speech and make last-minute revisions just as the event began.

After a few guest speakers had finished, Willem Kooyker, whom I had met the night before, began my introduction. I had given countless speeches before, and nervousness mixed with adrenaline always filled me the moment before I delivered any speech. This time was different. I felt comfortable and completely poised to do what I had come there to do. I took a moment to

pray like I always did. After Mr. Kooyker had finished
my introduction, amid loud applause, I finally made my
way to the podium.

> "I imagined my father next to me
> and recalled the dream that
> we both had come to share."

As I climbed the tall podium and looked out into the
crowd and saw hundreds of faces waiting for my first word,
I spaced out for a second and reminisced. I thought about
my mother back home who couldn't afford to be there.
I remembered my sister and all we had been through.
Finally, I imagined my father next to me and recalled the
dream that we both had come to share. With all that in
mind I gathered my composure and began:

> *Mentoring in its most profound role is the planting
> of seeds in the minds of future generations. Seeds
> bearing hope … the same hope that drives us all to
> pursue our dreams. Mentoring plants seeds that
> instill faith in the hearts of our youth, faith that tells
> them that although they can't see the finish line,
> know that one day they'll get there. They are seeds
> that completely erase the world's ideas about what is
> possible and what is impossible. And they are seeds that
> inspire boldness, boldness to take one's reality however
> grim and reshape it into one of infinite possibilities…*

I came back to Nebraska on a mission to close another chapter. I admit that I was tired. I couldn't remember the last time I got eight hours of sleep. And still playing catch up in most of my classes, there wouldn't be any time for sleep in the foreseeable future. The tan that I had obtained while in the Middle East quickly began to fade as I locked myself within my apartment walls.

The author speaking during the 2011 National Mentoring Summit in the Library of Congress's main reading room.

It is often said that the third year of law school is the least difficult. Some have even called for it to be eliminated altogether. I agree that it was the least difficult, but nonetheless there was still enough work to keep me more than busy. Wanting to mentally and physically lie down and take a break from it all, I couldn't help but stay diligent when I could taste the finish line.

From time to time my sister would send me pictures of my niece. It was amazing to see how much she had grown. As I witnessed her grow dramatically before my eyes, I wanted to do something for her to ensure that if anything happened to me tomorrow, she would have something, anything, that could be utilized to level her playing field. I had just the idea.

During the first few fiscal quarters of 2011, the economy had not yet found its legs. With a stock market that was so volatile, I thought it was the perfect time to take advantage in hope that it had bottomed out. My sister had saved a few thousand dollars for my niece from her insurance settlement after the accident. Notwithstanding the hectic times, I thought it would be the perfect moment to invest on her behalf, in hopes that since she was only six, by the time she reached the age of majority the global markets would have corrected themselves.

I was a block away from the wealth management firm. In my backpack was all the money my sister had saved for my niece, which had now been faithfully entrusted to me. I tightly held onto my backpack, like a halfback clutching a football while plowing into the end zone, as I walked down the street bearing the hopes of those closest to me on my shoulders.

As I stepped into the firm's office, the secretary gave me a curious look as if I had accidentally walked into the wrong suite. The secretary took my name as I sat down patiently waiting for my appointment. I thumbed through the latest issue of *Fortune* magazine, and then I heard "Mr. Garrett" come from an unfamiliar, clear and stern voice. I grabbed my belongings and entered the office of the financial manager.

After walking behind his desk he extended his arm and we shook hands. He was a handsome white gentleman, who likely had not yet seen the age of thirty. With perfectly cut blonde hair and blue eyes he seemed as if he would be more at home acting out a movie role than managing client's portfolios.

We were in the midst of small talk when he curiously asked, "What do you do?" I replied by telling him that I was in my last semester of law school. Ironically, he had long contemplated the same path before pursuing his current profession. His father was also a lawyer who practiced locally in the community. His father had provided him with the capital to start his own wealth management firm. It was the type of act that I yearned to be able to perform for my own children one day in the future. I hoped what I was doing now would give my niece similar opportunities someday.

I couldn't help but momentarily dwell on how things might have been different had my own father physically been there beside me along the way. Although I couldn't go back in time, I was there to help solidify my niece's future, in hopes that my small efforts might assist her in sidestepping the many pitfalls that my sister and I had once been forced to navigate. Maybe she wouldn't have to fill out sixty-seven scholarship applications like I had in order to receive a college education, at least not if I had anything to do with it.

The end of the semester began to approach, and with a heavy course load I stayed busy. Two classes in particular took up a large portion of my time. The classes were my mock trial and evidence courses. The law college had taken an original approach to teaching the two subjects by combining the courses into one extended lecture, with a chance to implement the learned material outside of the class with an adjunct professor once a week. Our adjunct professor was a federal magistrate judge. She was short with dirty blonde hair and always wore a distinct pair of glasses resting on the bridge of her nose.

With his niece Ania Dunn, the author poses for pictures at post-graduation reception hosted by local favorite eatery Big Mama's Kitchen.

At the end of the semester our entire class would organize into teams and would compete against each other during mock trials as the bulk of our final grade.

My partner's name was Leroy, and we were the only Black students in our entire class. Jointly pursuing his doctorate in psychology in conjunction with his law degree, he was one of smartest people I knew. With his excellent memory and quick wit combined with my advocacy and public speaking skills, I was determined to win our trial. Before I knew it the semester had drawn to a close and the day of our final trial had quickly come.

Walking into a large courtroom I was early, and the first of my classmates to arrive. I took the opportunity to study my notes and perfect my arguments. Our mock trial involved the case of a woman who had previously worked for a wealthy family as a maid. After an expensive $50,000 diamond brooch had come up missing in the house, my fictitious client, also her former employer, inquired as to its whereabouts, keeping in mind the maid's previous criminal record.

Partly offended and partly hurt, the maid walked off her job without prior notice, perplexed as to why she couldn't escape her criminal past. As a result of the incident she had been unable to solidify any gainful employment and was now suing my client for defamation of character.

Before long Leroy arrived along with the opposing counsel. During the mock trial the plaintiff's counsel would be acted out by a classmate named Josh. Josh was white, in his late twenties, and bald. Originally from California, he had something negative to say about Nebraska every time a chance was thrown his way. His passive-aggressive and over-confident demeanor had made him unpopular among our classmates. Leading up to the trial he had confidently predicted an easy victory.

Soon the presiding judge arrived along with the mock witnesses and jury, and the trial began.

Leroy led with a moving opening argument, and I congratulated him on a job well done as he sat back down next to me. Josh went next and performed better than I had expected him to. Next, Leroy and I took turns calling witnesses for the defense and performing cross-examinations on witnesses called by the plaintiff. Finally, it was time for the fictitious plaintiff to take the stand, and it was my turn to perform my cross-examination.

As I fired question after question at the plaintiff, she wouldn't give me an inch. Toward the end of my questioning it was time to attempt to enter in a key piece of evidence. In the fact pattern of the case the plaintiff had signed a loan agreement that she had defaulted on, which would not only make her appear desperate for money but would provide strong ammunition to further justify my client's suspicion as to the fate of the expensive diamond brooch.

As I attempted to lay the proper foundation in order to get the document admitted as evidence, the plaintiff played ignorant well. She even went as far as to deny any recognition of the document, but eventually would admit that she signed it in desperation. Ultimately, I was unable to admit the key piece of evidence.

As I retreated to my seat having lost the battle, I looked across the room at Josh who had a sly grin on his face. Something smelled fishy. After the last of the witnesses had been called, it could have been anyone's game. Before the closing argument was to begin we took a short recess. I sat down on a hard wooden bench in the back of the courtroom next to Leroy and discussed our remaining tactics.

Sitting just within hearing of Josh, I could hear Josh congratulating his witnesses. Listening more intently, we discovered that he had instructed the plaintiff to deny every question that I asked, regardless if it was true or not. He had cheated and had violated the code of academic honesty that was strictly enforced by our law school.

I remember that my father had been here before and that his legacy ran rich through my veins. Instead of telling on Josh, I was going to beat him at his own game. When the jury walked back into the room, it was time for our closing arguments, and I was first up.

I treated this moment like any other speech that I had given and prayed while imaging my father watching. I got up from my seat leaving my note cards behind on the table and walked in front of the jury box to begin the closing argument. For the next ten minutes I proceeded to pick apart the plaintiff's arguments making sure to point out that she was so desperate for money that she signed a loan agreement without checking to see what she signed. When I sat down, Leroy congratulated me and I felt confident with my performance.

Now it was Josh's turn. He stood in front of the jury with a pile of note cards in his hands and proceeded to counter our arguments. By the look of the jurors' faces it was hard to gauge whether or not they bought any of it. After Josh finished, he sat down and the judge read the jury instructions. Immediately thereafter the jury left the courtroom to deliberate.

Josh sat on the other side of the room next to the plaintiff acting as if he had the case in the bag. It wasn't long before the jury was done deliberating and had reached its verdict. The jury foreman handed the verdict to the judge, who immediately announced that Leroy and I had won!

As the judge released the jury, Josh was red in the face. As soon as they reached the door to exit the courtroom, Josh cried out in disbelief, "What was it? How did they win?"

The jury foreman awkwardly looked at the judge, as if hoping she would tell him he didn't have to reply. When she sat there as if equally interested in his response, he replied, "Their closing argument," and walked out of the courtroom.

Afterward, I grabbed a few beers with a couple of friends to celebrate the small victory, but with the majority of my remaining finals at hand the festivities were short lived.

For the next few weeks, I locked myself in my apartment writing papers and studying outlines. Every once in a while I would join Leroy and a few other friends in a study group at the law school. Before I knew it I would look up and realize that I was the only person left in the room. I labored until the janitor came inside the room to clean as a clear sign that it was time for me to go home.

Instead of going home to retire, I took caffeine pills to help me make the most out of the quiet morning hours. During the few hours of sleep that I managed to get, I started to have horrible dreams. The closer I got to the date of my last final, the worse my dreams became. It was as if something was determined to make sure that my dreams would never come to fruition.

I had been in a holding cell before, but this time felt different. Back in college although I had sat behind bars, in my heart there still had been hope. But at this moment all hope had escaped me. The deputy came and unlocked my cell door and guided me into the next building. Waiting outside of the courtroom sat family and friends, and I saw a group of disappointed faces.

It had been my last semester of law school. Everything I had worked so hard for was going to be snatched away. I couldn't believe that I had let everyone down. What I had done would land me in jail for years, and I had better get used to sitting on metal benches and peering out of iron bars, because this was my new reality. It was a reality that I had solely chosen to create and one where I would do anything to have a second chance at redemption. This was really it. I never in my wildest dreams could have imagined that things would ever turn out this way.

I woke up in a cold sweat with my heart pounding. I searched around in the dark for my cell phone and used its dim light to illuminate the darkness around me. And with a feeling of relief beyond measure, I realized that I was home in my bedroom, and it had only been a dream. It wasn't a nightmare, but a dream that was so vivid that I was sure it had been real. I knew that at so many points in my past, I shouldn't have made it this far.

With sorrow, I thought about the dreams of other young Blacks who had been caught up with the wrong crowd, or were at the wrong place at the wrong time. And as an unfortunate result, they would come to see their dreams disappear into oblivion. I had come to know so many who had become lost in the struggle.

> "I thought about the dreams of other young Blacks who had been caught up with the wrong crowd, or were at the wrong place at the wrong time."

I realized more than ever that I had been spared. I would never take my dream and the dream of my father before me for granted. What I had was precious and it was the only thing that gave me the ambition to make it through each day. My dream had been a gift infecting the deepest part of my consciousness as I slept and embedded itself in the safe of my soul. It was a dream that had saved me, and a dream that I realized was too powerful not to share.

My last final was in corporate law. The night before I had barely slept at all. I tossed and turned thinking about how close I was and how far I had come. I didn't want to mess anything up now.

Only a few hours later and with hardly a wink of sleep I sat in front of what would be the last examination of my academic career. Being one of three Blacks in a packed auditorium I remembered the plight of the forgotten. I remembered that more was contingent upon my success than merely my own well-being. With that in mind I tried my best to focus.

The proctor handed out the test booklet and shortly thereafter instructed the class to begin. For the next four hours all that could be heard throughout the auditorium was the sound of fingers typing furiously. While typing away, I attempted to regurgitate all that I had crammed into my clouded mind throughout the past semester. I fought off the feeling of fatigue, which like never before seemed to be compounded with a lifetime of drained perseverance.

It felt as if I had just started typing when the time was called and the proctor directed everyone to stop typing. If all went well it would be the end of seven years of continuous post-secondary education. I was just thankful to have made it this far. I was unsure regarding my ultimate performance. All I could do was wait and hope that the depletion of my last ounce of strength and determination had managed to get me across the finish line. In the meantime, I still had yet to put a dream to rest. There were a few more things I had left to do to honor my father's lingering legacy and finally let the pain and grief rest in peace.

CONCLUSION:

REBIRTH OF A DREAM

It was still fairly early in the morning when I pulled up in front of my old house on Twenty-Eighth Street. The celebration of my law school graduation had now died down for some time. I looked around curiously as drug feigns were already on the corner, punctual as they had always been. Dressed for a lunch meeting with Nebraska Congressman Lee Terry in a few hours, I stepped out of the car wearing a European cut mohair suit, a Brooks Brothers dress shirt, and a skinny tie. It was a stark contrast from the hole-filled garments I once wore while playing in the street I now stood on.

I intently eyed my childhood home filled with painful memories from my youth. I could see that it was now condemned. Frowning upon the neighborhood, it seemed as if no renovations had ever been able to erase its dark past. Wild weeds and uncut grass reached the height of my hips, while broken furniture and other litter was scattered throughout the entire property. It was an accurate representation of a neighborhood exhibiting dire signs of urban decay.

As I scanned the block, empty lots hugged the street, and boarded up homes outnumbered those that barely appeared to be inhabited. I felt like a cowboy walking into a ghost town in the Wild West, whose desertion masked a history that had been filled with misery. I pondered the fate of the other children whom I had seen so often briefly come and go through the doors of the many lifeless homes that now lined the street.

I sat down on the front steps of my former childhood home as strangers walked by curiously eyeing me as if I were wearing a Halloween costume on Labor Day. My eyes rested on the exact spot in the street where lightning had struck twenty-one years earlier. I remembered the moment I had inherited the dream of liberty from the tyranny of poverty. I had been passed the blueprint exposing the hidden paths out of the ghetto. Somehow I had been spared from becoming a casualty of the human imperfections inherent in democracy.

It had been so long since I had stood in the land of the lost. Yet, I still felt perfectly at home among the forgotten. I was still befuddled as to how I had avoided the mad grasp of overwhelming odds. It was clear that fate had been kind to me.

The real prospects of never escaping the gravity of the ghetto had been my kryptonite. I had always identified with the Wright brothers as I too forever longed to take flight. I had managed to position myself so that my children could bypass many of the barriers that I had endured in the environment I now sat in.

> "It had been so long since I had stood in the land of the lost."

While sitting on the concrete steps, I took a moment to remember where I had come from, in order to use it as fuel to propel myself further toward the epitome of what I could be. But there was one more thing I had to do before I could close this chapter once and for all.

A half hour later I stepped out of the car with time to spare before the sun reached its highest point in the afternoon sky. It had been seven years since I had last come to visit these hallowed grounds. I had been determined not to return empty handed or defeated.

The sound of machinery could be heard coming from the direction of those doing landscaping, as I struggled to remember the exact location. When I finally rediscovered the final resting place of my father, an emotional levy had broken as the tears freely flowed from hidden waterways within. I wiped away the dust and grass from the face of his headstone. Once again I had come bearing gifts.

I lined his headstone with a dozen red roses, signifying the wonders that are rarely found in full bloom protruding from desolate ground. I laid my cap and tassel down as a symbol of the sacrifices I had made to ensure that my father had not fallen in vain. I stood above my father's grave as all that physically remained of his memory.

As I gave his dream peace in its final resting place, my own dreams now branched off and took their place. Surrounded by the dead I still stood in the land of the living. One day I would rest among them, but in the meantime I wouldn't rest until circumstances forced me to rest among them. It was time to take the fire that had burned from inside me for so long and blaze a new trail—one that was originally mine.

I promised to tell our story and to serve as a beacon of inspiration to those similarly burdened by artificial limitations. How could I ever forget the forgotten? Simultaneously, I promised my father that my mother, sister, and niece would be taken care of as long as there was still breath in my body. I wiped the tears from my eyes with the back of my hand as I stood up, remembering my meeting that was quickly approaching.

I turned to walk away. It was the end of a long and difficult road, but I was optimistic about the future that lay ahead. Whatever that future may be, my past had prepared me beyond all measure, and I would endure through it all again without hesitation. Regardless of where life took me next, I would never forget. I was just thankful to have had the rare privilege to witness for a second time the enigma of hopeless ambition come to a gorgeous fruition. It was the recurring dilemma of a caged bird born with broken wings, who would somehow still manage to escape and soar above everything. I guess you could call it ... the rebirth of a dream.

About the Author

A native of Omaha, Nebraska, Ean Garrett received his Bachelor of Arts degree in Legal Communications and Political Science in 2008 from the historically Black college Howard University, located in Washington, D.C. While there he also served as the Founder/Director of the Howard University Chapter of Students for Barack Obama and also was a recipient of the Sallie Mae American Dream and Delegate Eleanor Holmes Norton Congressional Black Caucus Scholarships.

Ean holds a Juris Doctor degree from the University of Nebraska College of Law, which he received in 2011. He served as the President of the Black Law Students Association and Multi-Cultural Legal Society. Ean also successfully completed international coursework at CBL International's Law School in Dubai, U.A.E., in 2011/2012.

Ean has been heavily invested in furthering the causes of at-risk youth. Working with Metropolitan Community

College and the North Omaha Foundation, he coordinated conferences aimed at increasing the graduation rates of underprivileged demographics. Ean has previously served as a Congressional lobbyist on behalf of Trio/Upward Bound Programs. He also spends time working with programs that benefit inner-city youth.

Over the years Ean has served as a national spokesperson for MENTOR/National Mentoring Partnership, speaking on behalf of the organization at various venues throughout the country. As a result of his work in mentoring, Ean has been recognized in *Imagine* magazine, *Mott Mosaic* magazine, and has also been featured in the *Handbook of Youth Mentoring* by David L. Dubois. He continues to be a mentor, mentee, and advocate for the benefits of mentoring.